The Centers of Civilization Series

(COMPLETE LIST ON PAGE 193)

Dubrovnik

IN THE 14TH AND 15TH CENTURIES

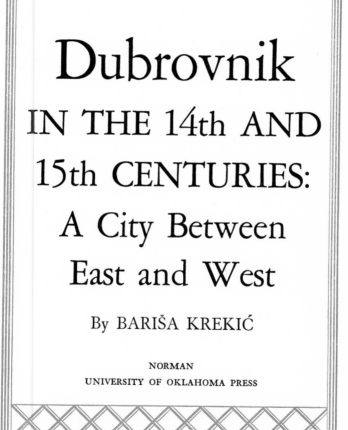

Dubrovnik

IN THE 14th AND 15th CENTURIES: A City Between East and West

By BARIŠA KREKIĆ

NORMAN
UNIVERSITY OF OKLAHOMA PRESS

By Bariša Krekić

Dubrovnik i Levant (1280–1460) (Belgrade, 1956).
Dubrovnik (Raguse) et le Levant au Moyen Age (Paris, 1961).
Dubrovnik in the 14th and 15th Centuries: A City Between East and West (Norman, 1972).

International Standard Book Number: 0–8061–0999–8

Library of Congress Catalog Card Number: 76–177340

Copyright 1972 by the University of Oklahoma Press, Publishing Division of the University. Composed and printed at Norman, Oklahoma, U.S.A., by the University of Oklahoma Press. First edition.

Dubrovnik in the 14th and 15th Centuries is Volume 30 in *The Centers of Civilization Series.*

Preface

THE purpose of this book is to present to the Western reader a city whose position and role for a thousand years was in many ways unique in Europe and whose contribution to the Mediterranean world was of great importance. This city, Dubrovnik—"The Jewel of the Adriatic"—has remained largely unknown to the Western public because of the language barrier. In fact, the vast majority of works on Dubrovnik have been published in Serbo-Croatian. The few publications in other languages are either antiquated or widely scattered.

The study of Dubrovnik is made possible by the existence in that city of a large and very valuable archive containing documents from the eleventh century on and also by the publication, in Yugoslavia, of a considerable number of monographs covering many aspects of Dubrovnik's life in various epochs. The research, however, is far from complete, and there is still no single, modern history of Dubrovnik. This volume does not intend to be one. Its aim is to show the city at a limited, though crucial, time of its development. Everything that is written here is based on my twenty years of work with published and unpublished materials in the historical archives of Dubrovnik and on the reading of monographs and articles concerning that city's past.*

Dubrovnik's importance comes from its role as a vital link in the exchange of men, goods, and ideas between East and West, particularly between the Balkans and Italy. This is why I shall attempt, while tracing Dubrovnik's past, to take into consideration events in the areas involved, stressing especially the developments in the Balkans, less well known to the Western reader.

It is with sincere gratitude and deep sadness that I mention here the name of the greatest historian of Dubrovnik, Professor Jorjo Tadić. As one of his long-time students, I was privileged to have the benefit of his help and advice while drafting the format of this book during the summer of 1969 in Dubrovnik. His valuable remarks and the manuscripts which he magnanimously offered me, although not yet published, helped greatly in the preparation of this work (the faults of which are, of course, entirely my own responsibility). Jorjo Tadić, unfortunately, died suddenly and prematurely in October, 1969, while this volume was being written. Thus Dubrovnik lost the scholar whose efforts, more than anybody else's, introduced its past into Mediterranean and European history and historiography.

I am also very much indebted to my friends and colleagues Professor Wayne S. Vucinich of Stanford University and Professor Sima M. Ćirković of Belgrade University, who made many useful suggestions for the improvement of this

*All quotations of texts from documents in this book are—unless otherwise indicated—from the historical archives in Dubrovnik.

book. My appreciation goes also to Mr. Zdravko Šundrica of the historical archives in Dubrovnik for checking a number of facts for me. It is a pleasure to mention here Mrs. Betty Messenger of Bloomington, Indiana, who kindly read the manuscript and painstakingly corrected the mistakes in my English.

B. Krekić

Contents

Maps

Dubrovnik

IN THE 14TH AND 15TH CENTURIES

I

Geography and Early History

T HE unique history and achievement of the small city
of Dubrovnik* is as much the result of the great ability
and the steady perseverance of its men and of historical events
and developments in the surrounding regions as it is the
product of the extremely favorable geographical location of
the city. Situated in the southern part of the eastern coast of the
Adriatic Sea, Dubrovnik has an open sea in front of it, while
at the same time it is in a position to have excellent communication with its hinterland. The development of this communication was slow but steady. Small roads going to the
nearby regions of Hum and Travunia eventually reached all
the way across the Balkan peninsula to the Danube, to
Thessalonica, and to Constantinople, their progress following

*It seems necessary to explain here the use of the names Dubrovnik,
Ragusium, and Ragusans in this book. The Slavic form Dubrovnik will be
introduced for the city in the second half of the twelfth century, when it is
mentioned for the first time in documents. The old Roman name Ragusium
will be used for the earlier epoch and later when it applies to the oldest
parts of the city. The name Ragusan(s) for citizens of Dubrovnik, as well as
the adjective Ragusan, will be used throughout, instead of Slavic forms, for
convenience.

3

channel, and that was the beginning of a new town, called Ragusium. The settlers, mostly of Roman origin, had as their neighbors the Slavs. Recent archaeological research and excavations in Dubrovnik itself, however, reveal that the rock on which the refugees from Epidaurus settled was inhabited a long time before their arrival.

The Roman inhabitants of Ragusium were forced almost immediately to deal with their Slavic neighbors on the mainland, for the rock could not support the newly arrived population; nor was the population able to find enough food and other necessities on the nearby seas. The Slavs were willing to allow the Ragusans to cultivate the land near the city in return for a tribute that the Ragusans would pay them. But Ragusium was not able to negotiate this matter alone. All the Dalmatian cities at the time were under Byzantine rule, and the Byzantine emperor ultimately had to agree to the arrangements made with the nearby Slavs. Thus it was Emperor Basil I who decided, in the second half of the ninth century, that the Ragusans would pay thirty-six golden *nomismata* a year to each of the princes of Zahumlje and Travunija. In return, the Ragusans were allowed to cultivate their possessions and vineyards on Slavic territory. This tribute, called *magarisium* or *mogoriš*, continued to be paid for centuries by Dubrovnik to the masters of the hinterland, the Serbians and the Bosnians, until the arrival of the Ottoman Turks.

By the middle of the ninth century, Ragusium was already a fortified city of considerable importance on the southern Adriatic. In 866–67 it was able to withstand fifteen months of siege by Arabs from southern Italy, and two years later

6

the Ragusans themselves participated in an expedition of the Frankish army against the Arabs. On orders from Constantinople, Ragusan ships helped transport Croatian and other Slavic troops from the eastern to the western coast of the Adriatic in preparation for an attack on Arab-held Bari. This certainly is sufficient proof that the city was relatively strong as a fortification and important on the sea.

The eleventh century, however, greatly changed the situation on the Adriatic as a whole and on its eastern shores in particular. These changes for the first time involved Ragusium—until then a city exclusively under Byzantine authority—in political activities and upheavals which had important consequences for its further development. In the year 1000 the Venetians launched their first drive to conquer Dalmatia with the expedition of the Doge Pietro II Orseolo. Having obtained the blessing of the Byzantine emperor, Basil II, busy with other, more pressing matters, Orseolo sailed into Dalmatia with a fleet and was able to bring into submission a series of northern and central Dalmatian islands and cities, while others were conquered by force. Thus he established the Venetian presence from the Quarnero to the island of Lastovo (Lagosta), an area including the cities of Zadar (Zara), Trogir (Tragurium), and Split (Spalatum). Even the Croatian king, Kresimir III, had to pay his respects to the Venetian doge, make an alliance with him, and give him his son as a hostage. Ragusium, too, submitted to the Venetian domination for the first time in its history. However, this lasted only a short time and then Byzantine domination was restored in the city. By 1030, Ragusan ships were taking part in an expedition led by the Byzantines against the Arabs

7

in southern Italy, and a little later a Byzantine *strategos*, or general, is mentioned as the head of a Byzantine military-administrative unit, the *Theme*, in Ragusium.

The situation in the Adriatic in the eleventh century was changing not only because of the Venetian expansion but also because of the appearance in southern Italy of a new power, the Normans. Having established his state in southern Italy between 1059 and 1071, Robert Guiscard embarked immediately on a rapid expansion toward the East. His policy brought the Normans to the Dalmatian coast and to the Epirus. The Byzantine Empire had been weakened substantially by fifty years of rule by a civilian aristocracy which disregarded military needs and by the catastrophic battle of Manzikert in 1071 in which the Seljuk army utterly defeated the Byzantines and captured their emperor. The empire was completely unable to defend its far-removed western possessions. Thus, in the second half of the eleventh century, the Byzantine presence in the Adriatic consisted of theoretical claims to its sovereignty there rather than its practical enforcement. Consequently the Dalmatian towns and Ragusium increasingly took positions in accordance with their own immediate interests and so established their own independent political life.

The weakness of the Byzantine Empire became especially apparent when a Byzantino-Norman war broke out in 1081. Unable to withstand the Norman attacks and to defend the Epirote coast on their own, the Byzantines asked the Venetians to help them. The Venetians accepted the invitation, because by helping the Byzantines they were also achieving one of the most important and constant goals of their own policy: the prevention of one single power from establishing its rule on both sides of the Adriatic and on the Strait of Otranto. Such a threat was always a nightmare to the Venetians, and they were only too eager to help prevent the Normans from achieving their aims. But the Venetians were too shrewd as politicians not to take advantage of the Byzantine need for help, and they made the Byzantines pay a very high price for it. In 1082 the new Byzantine emperor, Alexius I Comnenus, granted extensive privileges to Venice, most important of which were trade concessions, which laid the foundation of the subsequent enormous Venetian economic expansion and colonial empire in the eastern Mediterranean. This expansion, in turn, had important effects on the history of Dubrovnik, as we shall see later. The thing to note now is that during the war of 1081–85, with the Byzantines and Venetians on one side and the Normans on the other, the Ragusans turned against their masters until then, the Byzantines, and joined the Normans. This is certainly proof of a much-increased independence, not only in action, but also in political thinking in Ragusium at the time, since this switch of allegiances was accompanied by a brief recognition of Norman authority in Ragusium.

This independence was probably enhanced by other happenings in the Dalmatian area. The Croatian state, during the long rule of King Stephen (c. 1030–58), was struggling to obtain the Dalmatian cities from the Venetians and was, in part, successful. A large measure of this success was achieved by Stephen's successor, King Peter Kresimir IV (1058–74), who managed to obtain from the Byzantine emperor the right to govern the Dalmatian cities. However, after Peter

Kresimir's death the situation changed. Croatia started on the road of rapid decline, marked by the decision of Emperor Alexius I in 1085 to entrust the Venetians with the rule of the Dalmatian cities. The Venetians enforced this imperial decision after the death of the Croatian king, Zvonimir (1075–89). A new element was then introduced into Croatian and Dalmation affairs—the Hungarians. After several years of fighting and political tribulations, which culminated in the defeat of the Croatian forces by the Hungarians in 1097, the Hungarian king, Koloman, managed to impose his rule on Croatia and Dalmatia in 1102. He was recognized and accepted as Croatian king and, although the legal and symbolic elements indicating the continuity of Croatian statehood were preserved, for all practical purposes Hungarian rule was imposed. Thus a strong, new state emerged on the eastern Adriatic coast.

These events did not immediately affect Ragusium, too far removed to the south, but they were to have important consequences later. However, in the eleventh century another region, nearer to Ragusium, was witnessing events of great significance. In Dioclea, or Zeta, rebellions against Byzantine rule began in 1035 to gain momentum, and in 1040 a Byzantine *strategos* from Ragusium was captured by the rebels, led by their chief, Vojislav. Byzantine attempts to put down the rebellion ended in defeat, and finally they gave up, thus allowing the formation of a new state in Zeta. Vojislav extended his authority over Travunija as well and thus became the immediate neighbor of Ragusium. This situation continued under the rule of his son, Michael (c. 1052–81). Michael, profiting by disorders in the region of Raška, north-east of Zeta, managed to conquer, albeit temporarily, that territory, heretofore under Byzantine domination, and thus created a large state in the hinterland of Ragusium. He obtained the royal crown from Pope Gregory VII in 1077. The state of Zeta was becoming increasingly a new element that all Ragusan political calculations had to take into serious account.

Meanwhile the city of Ragusium itself was gaining strength and importance throughout the eleventh century. There were many events contributing to this growth, and one of the most significant occurred in 1022. The pope decided to elevate the Ragusan bishopric to the status of archbishopric, placing under its jurisdiction a large area from the Neretva River in the north to the Bojana River in the south and going deep into the Balkan interior. The act, however, provoked sharp reactions from the ecclesiastical see in Split and later led to a bitter clash with the newly established archbishopric in Bar (1089), in Zeta, which lasted two centuries. Nevertheless, the pope's decision was, beyond any doubt, a major event for the Ragusans.

Another very important indication of Ragusium's growth and development in the first half of the eleventh century is the first mention of the local nobility in 1023, although this social group was still far removed from the later Ragusan patriciate. There was also, from the tenth century on, a steady increase in the Slavic population within Ragusium. This was brought about by the development of the city, which resulted in the increase of jobs and the attraction of more manpower to Ragusium, mainly from the nearby Slavic regions. The demographic growth of Ragusium was made and could only have been made possible through an increase in the Slavic segment of the city's population, and this situation prevailed throughout the history of Dubrovnik.

The twelfth century was a period of particular importance in the history and development of Ragusium. After the short interlude of Norman domination (1081–85), the city returned to Byzantine protection. There were other brief spans of time when Norman authority was recognized (for example, in 1172 and again in 1189–90, as well as at the turn of the twelfth and the thirteenth centuries). In 1171 the city was conquered and occupied briefly by the Venetian fleet on its way to fight Byzantium in the East, but Ragusium remained in the twelfth century essentially a city under Byzantine protection. It was obviously very convenient for the Ragusans to be the protégés of an old and prestigious, if weak, state which was too far removed to try to impose any real domination on the city. Confronted with the growing power of Venice, with the newly emerged but strong Hungarian presence in Dalmatia, and with the Norman state in southern Italy at its apogee, Ragusium thought it wise to cling to the old allegiances.

In the first half of the twelfth century, the Ragusans developed a considerable maritime trade and commercial navigation. Of course, their presence on the sea, as previously mentioned, was almost as old as the city itself, but it is from the middle of the twelfth century that its importance increased rapidly, according to preserved documentary evidence. In 1143 the first Ragusan traveled, probably on a Venetian ship, to Cyprus, Accon, and Constantinople. Much more significant was a series of treaties between Dubrovnik and Italian cities: Molfetta (1148), Pisa (1169), Ancona (1188), Fano

(1199), Monopoli and Bari (1201), Termoli (1203), and Bisceglie (1211). All of these treaties were meant to facilitate trade between the ports, and they show that Dubrovnik was becoming a serious commercial partner to a large number of Italian cities. This importance of Dubrovnik is further confirmed by the first privilege that the city obtained from a Byzantine emperor. It was in 1192 that Emperor Isaak II Angelus issued a chrysobull to Dubrovnik by which, among other things, he allowed the Ragusans free trade in his empire.

It was still difficult for the Ragusans to try to penetrate deeper into the Balkan hinterland. Events in this region in the first half of the twelfth century were less than reassuring. After the death of Constantine Bodin (1081–c. 1101), who succeeded King Michael of Zeta, the center of the struggle for Serbian independence shifted increasingly northeastward, toward Raška, and this was accompanied by prolonged internal conflicts. Apart from these developments, unfavorable to possible contacts between Dubrovnik and the Balkans, there was little reason at this time for the Ragusans to be eager to visit those areas, for the economic attractions of the lands did not develop until later.

It was in the last quarter of the twelfth century that the Ragusans started looking for ways to penetrate more efficiently into the Balkan hinterland, and two agreements resulted. In Serbia (Raška) the new ruler—who had emerged from a prolonged period of internal strife and who had managed to stabilize the situation and to lay down the fundamentals of an enduring dynasty—waged a war to conquer Dubrovnik but was unsuccessful. So Grand Zhupan Stephen Nemanja

(c. 1169–96) came to terms with Dubrovnik and made peace in 1186, at the same time granting the Ragusans the right to safe and free trade in Serbia. Another treaty, with Bosnia in 1189, promised the Ragusans freedom of movement and freedom from customs fees in Bosnia, a region which was only beginning to take shape as a state under its ruler, or ban, Kulin (c. 1180–c. 1204). With these two treaties, the gates of the Balkan peninsula opened wider to Dubrovnik. Although Ragusan merchants did not avail themselves of this new opportunity at the time, the two treaties were very important steps on a course which would eventually lead Dubrovnik to its greatest prosperity. It is in the treaty with Bosnia in 1189 that the first mention of the Slavic form of the city name, Dubrovnik, is found.

Meanwhile several processes of economic and social development were going on inside the city. With increased trade, the pace of the economic growth of Dubrovnik was bound to be intensified, and evidently the profits were not shared equally by all segments of the population. It is apparent from the above-mentioned treaties that there existed in Dubrovnik in the twelfth century an increasingly distinguishable group of families whose role in the political life of the city was predominant. These were the richest, most influential families, belonging to the *nobiles*, who would later join the patrician ranks. Another very clear sign of the great development of the city is the first mention, in 1181, of the denomination *Communitas Ragusii*, "the Commune of Ragusium." Dubrovnik was apparently engaged on a road of development similar to the one followed by many Italian and other Western cities, toward a patrician-ruled city-state.

Probably the most important conclusion that can be drawn from Dubrovnik's twelfth-century history is that the city for the first time began playing a certain role in East-West relations. Through its commercial treaties with Italian cities on the one hand and through the privileges and treaties with Byzantium, Serbia, and Bosnia on the other, Dubrovnik became a point of contact, of conjunction, between the two areas. It is true that at this early stage the city's role was limited, compared to later times. Dubrovnik still lacked the means and the experience to engage in more intense exchange activities, and foreign merchants had not yet discovered the possibilities of the city. But the time would come, and very soon, when the start made in the twelfth century would boom into a flourishing activity, bringing enormous profits to all concerned and transforming Dubrovnik into a real focus of East-West relations, not only for economic but for cultural and other reasons too.

This transformation was already beginning in the thirteenth century. The century opened with events which profoundly altered the political balance of the whole Mediterranean world, particularly its eastern part, and which most directly affected Dubrovnik. The Venetians, who had been increasing their positions and strength in the Byzantine Empire throughout the twelfth century, had become disillusioned with Byzantine governments in the last third of the century and were looking for an opportunity to strengthen even further their grip not only on the Byzantine economy but on its government and policy as well. The Fourth Crusade proved to be the ideal chance for the realization of these Venetian plans. The old, almost blind, but extremely shrewd and energetic doge, Enrico Dandolo, profiting by a number of circumstances, managed to convince the Crusaders first into conquering the Dalmatian city of Zadar, held by the Hungarians, for Venice and then into going to Constantinople instead of Egypt. There they conquered the Imperial City and ultimately abolished the Byzantine Empire on the Bosporus in 1204. Of course, Venice profited most from these events. It established a real colonial empire, stretching through Dalmatia, Corfu, Crete, and Euboea to Constantinople itself, where the Venetians had their own quarter and complete political, ecclesiastical, and economic predominance in the newly established Latin Empire.

Venice's new position as one of the leading European powers and beyond doubt as the most powerful Mediterranean state put Dubrovnik in an unpleasant position. Its protector, the Byzantine Empire, had disappeared, albeit temporarily, and there was no one in the vicinity on whom Dubrovnik could rely against Venice. Finally, the power of Venice, with its colonies both to the north and to the south of Dubrovnik and its powerful fleets sailing the Adriatic and the Mediterranean, apparently unbeatable, forced Dubrovnik into submission to Venetian domination in 1205.

The only possible alternative to this submission perhaps would have been the surrender of Dubrovnik to the vigorously expanding Serbian state, always eager to obtain part of the Adriatic coast. For the Ragusans, however, this was out of the question. The refusal to become part of any state in the hinterland, be it Serbia, Bosnia, or, later, the Ottoman Empire, was one of the first principles of Ragusan policy for centuries, in spite of the tributes paid to all of these states.

In medieval Dubrovnik the antagonistic attitude toward the conquering appetites of the Slavic states of the interior was caused, no doubt, by the desire of the Ragusans to preserve their communal structure and autonomy, for which the Slavic states could be expected to have little sympathy; by different social structures and religious traditions; by different economic and political orientations and aims; and, at the early stages, by ethnic differences, at least among the ruling groups.

Having accepted Venetian domination, Dubrovnik had to put up with its consequences as well. The city had to agree to having a Venetian patrician as *comes*, or count, at its head. The rights of this Venetian count in Dubrovnik and his role in the political life of the city were considerable in the earlier stages of Venetian domination, but later were curtailed little by little by the domestic aristocracy. It is important to note that, although Dubrovnik became a vital focal point of Venetian commercial navigation and a precious base for the Venetian navy, it was never occupied by Venetian soldiers. The city was always free of foreign troops. Moreover, the local nobility managed to preserve its position in the government of the city, the position it had increasingly taken for itself during the twelfth century. Thus the Venetian count was flanked by Ragusan patricians, members of rich families, who little by little organized themselves into three governmental bodies: the *Consilium Maius* (Major Council), the *Consilium Minus* (Minor Council), and the *Consilium Rogatorum* (the Senate).

Venetian overlordship imposed some hardships and limitations on the Ragusans, particularly in their maritime trade.

For example, they could not come to Venice with more than four small ships a year and they were not allowed to do any business with foreigners in Venice. At the same time, the Venetians tried stubbornly to ensure a special and privileged situation for their merchants in Dubrovnik but were only partly successful.

On the other hand, Dubrovnik profited by some aspects of the Venetian domination. The mere presence of Venetian ships in the harbor was, no doubt, a considerable contribution to Dubrovnik's economic life. The Venetian ships used Dubrovnik as a port in which they completed their crews before going on to the Levant. They sometimes exchanged entire crews upon returning from long eastern trips and took provisions before venturing toward the less than hospitable shores of the Ionian and Mediterranean seas. For the Venetian war fleets cruising in the Adriatic or going to the Levant, Dubrovnik was also an extremely useful harbor, especially when, on Venetian orders, an arsenal was organized there in 1329. But Dubrovnik profited also from Venetian protection of its ships on the seas and in foreign ports. In addition, the Ragusans found that Venice was a city where it was always relatively easy to recruit specialists of all kinds which were greatly needed in Dubrovnik at the time. Venice was also a center of information, which the Ragusans were always eager to acquire.

More importantly, Venetian diplomatic protection proved particularly welcome when the Serbians showed signs of aggression aimed at conquering Dubrovnik and absorbing it into their state. Serbia had gone through important developments in the first two decades of the thirteenth century. In

1217 its ruler, Grand Zhupan Stephen (1196–c. 1228), obtained the royal crown from the pope and thus became the first Serbian king (he is called "Stephen the First Crowned"). At the same time, in 1219, the king's brother, the able monk-diplomat Rastko-Sava Nemanjić, managed to obtain from the patriarcate of Nicaea the autonomy of the Serbian church, hitherto under the jurisdiction of the archbishopric of Okhrida. Sava himself was consecrated in 1219 as autocephalous archbishop of Serbia, and thus the independence of the Serbian church was assured.

During the reign of Stephen's two successors, Stephen Radoslav (c. 1228–c. 1234) and Stephen Vladislav (c. 1234–43), the tensions between Dubrovnik and Serbia slowly mounted as the young Serbian state went through internal upheavals. These tensions later culminated in a war between Dubrovnik and Serbia in 1252, during the rule of King Stephen Uroš I (1243–76). This king embarked on a dynamic policy of expansion, and the conflict with Dubrovnik was almost inevitable. A number of other wars followed, to be ended by 1327–28 with the preservation of Dubrovnik's independence and the establishment of durable good relations between the two powers.

It was during these conflicts that Venetian protection proved to be very precious to Dubrovnik. The Venetians, indeed, never let down their protégés. They constantly intervened diplomatically with Serbian rulers and noblemen in favor of Dubrovnik. Of course, the Venetian attitude was not dictated by sentiment but by realistic political appraisals and calculations. The Venetians knew, in fact, that it would be very inconvenient for themselves if a vigorous new power like Serbia emerged in a major way on the Adriatic and obtained a city whose inhabitants were skilled on the sea, while Venice would simultaneously lose one of its very important bases. For Dubrovnik the main goal was to stay independent from Serbia and remain available for the role of middleman between East and West, which proved to be its true vocation.

Dubrovnik started playing this role in the vastly changed world of the thirteenth century on a much larger scale and with much more determination than in the previous century. In addition to the treaties with Italian cities, Dubrovnik established relations in the first part of the century with the Despotate of Epirus, as well as with Bulgaria and Thessalonica. It must be emphasized also that the wars between Dubrovnik and Serbia in the second half of the thirteenth and the beginning of the fourteenth century did not sever the commercial and human ties between the two regions. The wars, in fact, were only temporary interruptions in an otherwise steadily increasing flow of contacts of all kinds. Similarly, the relations between Dubrovnik and Bosnia were excellent. The Bosnian ban, Matej Ninoslav (1232–50) promised freedom and protection to Ragusan merchants in his country.

The interest of the Ragusans in good relations with the states of the Balkan hinterland suddenly acquired a new dimension toward the middle of the thirteenth century, when mining was started at Brskovo, in Serbia. The beginning of Serbian mining was largely due to the arrival of German miners (Saxons), mainly from Hungary. It spread and developed very rapidly in Serbia and in a very short time brought new wealth to the Serbian rulers, new power to the state, and new and unexpected profits to the Ragusans. For the Ragusans, having sensed from the outset all the implications of the new activity in Serbia, immediately started taking part in it. Although the citizens of Kotor (a town belonging to Serbia, south of Dubrovnik) played an important part in Serbian mining and trade until the second half of the fourteenth century, the Ragusans established themselves very early as the main transporters of Serbian silver, copper, lead, iron, and other minerals to the Adriatic. They obtained leases on mines and later became owners of many of them. Their role in the development of mining in Serbia was extremely valuable. They were the chief middlemen in the exportation of minerals to the West and thereby stimulated the production of the mines in Serbia itself. Also, the increased prosperity of Serbia enabled the Ragusans to increase their imports of Western goods to that country.

Of course, all of this trading went through the city of Dubrovnik and its harbor, and the profits it brought to Dubrovnik, through customs fees and in other ways, were immense. Very soon merchants and captains of other nationalities began taking part in the shipping of minerals to Italy, but the Ragusans always retained the leading position in communications with the hinterland. It is hard to exaggerate the importance of Serbian and, a little later, Bosnian mining to the development of Dubrovnik. The rapid and big profits the Ragusans made in their activity as middlemen for the Balkan mines, enabled them to quicken the urbanization of their city (see Chapter III) and to increase their hygienic and cultural standing as well (see Chapters IV and V). At the same time, and very importantly, the new, brisk, and booming economic activity brought into the city large numbers of men needed as manpower. These men were Balkan Slavs, and the ensuing demographic growth was, in fact, the slavicization of Dubrovnik.

Thus at the end of the thirteenth century there seemed to be many bright prospects for Dubrovnik. Mining was developing and so was Ragusan participation in it; the city was prospering and was being urbanized; Ragusan ships pushed farther and farther out onto the Mediterranean. Still there were darker spots in the picture. Venetian-imposed limitations continued to exist; Serbian expansion remained dangerous for Dubrovnik; Bosnia was on the move with unpredictable consequences; Hungary was struggling to stabilize its position in Dalmatia; and a new power had taken over in southern Italy—the Angevins. The future must have looked promising but certainly not overly reassuring to the Ragusans at the turn of the century.

II

Politics and Economics in the Fourteenth and Fifteenth Centuries

THE political orientation and activity of Dubrovnik in the first half of the fourteenth century was in response to two major influences: its economic interests and the Venetian overlordship of the city. Economic interests, notably those of Ragusan commerce, resulted in a great increase of political contacts with the Balkan hinterland. The involvement of the Ragusans in Serbian mining stimulated the patricians, when sitting in governmental councils and deciding on political questions, to try to establish and preserve good relations with Serbian authorities. The same was true, a little later, of relations with Bosnia. But in both cases things did not go smoothly all the time.

On the other hand, Venetian presence and the limitations that the Venetians imposed on Ragusan shipping and maritime trade, although not of a drastic nature, certainly can be taken as a second influence causing the Ragusan government to direct its efforts increasingly toward the Balkans. Thus a fortunate coincidence took place. At a time when the Venetians, as protectors of Dubrovnik, were trying to limit the city's maritime trade, Dubrovnik was able to profit by expansion in a new direction, and this offered the basis for its spectacular development in the next several centuries. The Venetians—in what seems to be one of the few mistakes they ever made in their political and economic calculations—never quite grasped the importance of the new activity in the Balkans and consequently never took much advantage of it.

It was not always easy, however, for Dubrovnik to preserve its contacts and position in the Balkans, particularly in Serbia. We have seen that wars between the two states were not rare in the second half of the thirteenth century. With the arrival of King Stephen Uroš II Milutin (1282–1321) on the Serbian throne, a new era of Serbian expansion began. This expansion was mainly directed toward the southeast, toward the rich Byzantine lands, but Milutin did not neglect other areas, including those in the vicinity of Dubrovnik. Twice during his reign Dubrovnik was at war with Serbia, in 1301–1302 and in 1317–18. Both times the Ragusans, with Venetian help, managed to preserve their independence, and the city of Kotor remained Serbia's main outlet on the Adriatic. Milutin's son, King Stephen Uroš III Dečanski (1321–31), made the last Serbian effort to conquer Dubrovnik, with a war waged in 1327–28. But the results for Serbia were not better than in the previous attempts, and the Venetians once more proved to be unswervingly on the side of Dubrovnik.

After this, Serbian-Ragusan relations changed completely. In 1331 the greatest Serbian medieval ruler, King—and, from 1345, Emperor—Stephen Dušan (1331–55), began to govern. His orientation and the orientation that he gave to the Serbian state was completely toward the south and southeast. Dušan was eager to conquer rich Byzantine lands and cities and was fully supported by his nobility. Dušan desired also, albeit later, to replace the vacillating Byzantine Empire, torn by internal strife and economic weaknesses, with a strong, prosperous, and aggressive Serbian state. In the realization of this scheme he was very successful. His armies conquered not only all of Macedonia to the walls of Thessalonica and large portions of Thrace, but also Epirus, Thessaly, and other Greek territories. Thus, an empire was formed which stretched from the Danube in the north to the Gulf of Corinth in the south and from the vicinity of Dubrovnik in the west to that of the Maritsa River in the east. But the Serbians never took Constantinople and thus never fully achieved their ruler's dream.

Because of his eastern orientation, Dušan was willing to neglect his western lands. This can be seen, among other things, in his relations with Dubrovnik. Dušan abandoned completely his predecessor's policy of trying to conquer the city. On the contrary, he did his best to establish friendly relations with the Ragusans. They, of course, were only too eager to accept and support such policies. This new atmosphere in Serbian-Ragusan relations was manifested most clearly in two events: the selling, in 1333, of the peninsula of Pelješac, northwest of the city, to the Ragusans by Dušan and his personal visit to Dubrovnik in 1350. Pelješac was a valuable addition to the small Ragusan territory.

Dušan's friendship, in general, meant even more. It enabled the merchants of Dubrovnik to engage with a new sense of security in trading, investments, and other enterprises in Serbia. Dušan's good will can be seen, in particular, from the charter that he gave to the city in 1349 and which became the model for all Serbian privileges given to Dubrovnik in the next hundred years. The Ragusans were allowed to circulate safely and freely with their merchandise throughout the emperor's lands, provided they paid customs fees. They were also permitted to travel through Serbia to other countries, on condition that they would carry arms "neither to the Bulgarians, nor to Bassarab's land, nor to the Hungarians, nor into Bosnia, nor to the Greeks, nor anywhere else in foreign lands." Never before had Ragusan activity in Serbia attained such intensity as in Dušan's time, and, of course, Dubrovnik profited tremendously by it.

In turn, Serbia benefited from the increased trade and the export of its goods, particularly minerals, through Dubrovnik to the West. For, while it is correct to say that Serbia, in culture, religion, and even in political and military methods, was oriented very much toward Byzantium and was influenced by that empire, it is also true that economically Serbia thrived on its contacts and trade with the West, not the East. There is scarcely any information indicating the existence of Serbian trade with Byzantium and even the little that there is shows Western, primarily Ragusan, merchants carrying it on. It was the exportation of its minerals and other goods to the West, Italy in particular, that provided the basis for Serbia's wealth, which was used to support the victorious Serbian armies and to build magnificent churches and monasteries, decorated with frescoes which to this day remain among the most brilliant achievements of medieval European art. And in this all-important trade with the West, Dubrovnik played an indispensable part.

A somewhat parallel development—although on a smaller

scale—was taking place in the relations between Dubrovnik and Bosnia. In the first half of the fourteenth century, under Ban Stephen II Kotromanić (1314–53), Bosnia experienced constitutional stabilization and economic progress. In the 1330's mining began in Bosnia, and it very quickly transformed the life of the country. The Ragusans immediately took key positions in this mining activity, as they had in Serbia, exporting silver, lead, iron, and other minerals to the sea and importing Western goods to the newly enriched Bosnian market. Despite the previous long presence of Ragusan merchants in Bosnia, this region could not be compared with Serbia in its importance to the Ragusans. However, their involvement and interest in Bosnia steadily increased and became a very important additional element of Ragusan prosperity.

As part of the Venetian domain, Dubrovnik continued to have lively contacts of all sorts with Venice. But this did not prevent the Ragusans from working very assiduously at the furthering of ties with other Italian cities, particularly those of southern Italy, as well as Ancona and Florence. All this resulted from Dubrovnik's new role as middleman between the Balkans and Italy. The currents of East-West trade, which, through Dubrovnik, carried Balkan minerals and other goods to the Italian markets, and the corresponding currents of West-East trade, which, again through Dubrovnik, carried Italian and other Western goods into the Balkans, brought about a need for the establishment, preservation, and further improvement of close relations between Dubrovnik and various Italian cities and regions, and the Ragusans always worked diligently at this task.

Good relations with the Croatian populations of Dalmatia, under Venetian rule, which existed from previous times, continued in the fourteenth century. Large numbers of Croatians from neighboring lands had moved into Dalmatian cities and to the islands off the coast. There is no doubt that by the fourteenth century not only was the countryside Croatian—as it had been for many centuries—but the islands and the bulk of the city populations were too. Only the ruling groups of local patricians remained predominantly Roman, which they stressed now more than ever. However, while on the surrounding large estates great Croatian feudal families (Šubić, Nelipčić, and others) held sway, the political situation in the urban centers was more complicated. Foreign intervention—notably that of the Venetians and the Hungarians as each tried to expand—constantly pitted different segments of the population against one another. Furthermore, the Croatian nobility kept changing sides or trying to take the cities for themselves. The cities, however, were eager to preserve their internal autonomies of old date. It is not surprising, for example, that the ancient city of Zadar became the scene of a series of violent rebellions against Venice's rule in the thirteenth and fourteenth centuries.

Still, all these events and difficulties did not prevent the Dalmatian cities and Dubrovnik from maintaining constant and excellent ties. It was through Dalmatia that Ragusan ships sailed to Venice and back, and the cities of Split, Trogir, Šibenik, Zadar, and others attracted Ragusan merchants. Many inhabitants of these cities not only visited Dubrovnik, but also settled there permanently.

The role of newcomers in Dubrovnik's life was very important, as has already been seen. Among these newcomers, two groups can be distinguished. One consisted of Slavic-speaking foreigners who came from nearby Slavic lands—Serbia, Bosnia, and Dalmatia. The other was made up of foreigners who came from more distant lands and spoke different languages. Of these non-Slavic newcomers, the most numerous and most important were, of course, the Italians, and among them the Venetians. They numbered in the hundreds in the fourteenth century. Some of them came with entire families and settled in Dubrovnik. Others lived for prolonged periods of time in the city. Sometimes wealthy merchants from Venice, Florence, or other Italian cities sent several generations of their families to work in Dubrovnik without ever settling there permanently. For centuries southern Italians came to Dubrovnik with particular frequency.

The vast majority of Italians, however, came to Dubrovnik only for brief business stays. After taking care of their affairs, ships, merchandise, or money, they left again, returning perhaps in a few weeks or months for another brief visit. It is interesting to note that in the first half of the fourteenth century the famous Florentine banking houses of Bardi, Peruzzi, and Acciaiuoli had representatives in Dubrovnik and did business from there with nearby Kotor, with southern Italy, Venice, and other regions. Their presence and activity certainly helped improve banking methods and exchange practices in Dubrovnik itself and presumably, through Ragusans, in the Balkan hinterland.

Besides the Italians, there were many other foreigners in fourteenth- and fifteenth-century Dubrovnik. Greeks, Levantines, and Albanians came to the city, and in the second half of the fourteenth century there were small groups of Frenchmen. In the fifteenth century Catalan merchants appeared in greater numbers. Jews arrived in Dubrovnik from various places, such as Italy, Albania, and Greece. The first mention of a Jew in the city is that of a doctor, a Christianized Jew, in the middle of the fourteenth century. In the second half of that century there were in Dubrovnik a number of Jewish merchants from Albania and Malta and later from Padova and Crete. A "Giudecca" is mentioned at this time in Dubrovnik, probably a Jewish quarter, situated in the eastern suburb of the city. However, since there were very few Jews in Dubrovnik and there is no proof that any had settled permanently in the city, it seems probable that Giudecca designated the place where foreign Jewish merchants lived while visiting Dubrovnik.

At the beginning of the fifteenth century Jews expelled from France and southern Italy started arriving in Dubrovnik, but it was only at the end of the century that the Jewish element in Dubrovnik became important. After their expulsion from Spain (1492) and Portugal (1498), many Jews escaped toward the East, particularly toward Ottoman lands. Many of these refugees traveled on Ragusan ships to Italian, Greek, and Dalmatian ports and to Dubrovnik itself. From Dubrovnik part of these Jews continued their journey to the East, into Balkan Ottoman regions, while others remained in the city, creating a colony there which lasted until recent times.

Except for the Catalans, foreigners were attracted to Dubrovnik mainly by the carrying trade between Italy and the Balkans which passed through the city. Their main interest was to obtain a share in this profitable business. Very rarely, however, did they go into the interior, because of the rugged country, the language barrier, and other factors. This meant that the Ragusans, who spoke the language, were as important to the foreign merchants in Dubrovnik as they were to the Serbians and Bosnians in carrying on this flow of trade. The foreigners, particularly the Italians, played a major role in the financing of Ragusan expeditions to the hinterland through credits that they gave to Ragusan merchants, and it can be safely assumed that the major portion of Balkan minerals and Italian goods were carried on the Adriatic Sea on foreign, not Ragusan, ships.

The presence of all these foreigners, although usually temporary, was of great value to Dubrovnik, not only because of the direct economic benefits, but also because many of these individuals undoubtedly brought with them superior commercial techniques, craftsmanship, navigational skills, and the like. Also there were among the foreigners many men with special skills—physicians, notaries, pharmacists, shipbuilders, architects—whom the Ragusan government brought over from Italy and whose impact on the new environment was certainly very important (see Chapters III, IV, V). The point which must be stressed in connection with the presence of all these persons in Dubrovnik is that, through the Ragusans, their influence extended far beyond the city into the Balkans.

The more important group of foreigners to the long-range development of Dubrovnik, however, were the Slavic-speaking peoples from the Balkans and from Dalmatia. Dubrovnik's booming economy demanded more and more manpower and offered increasing opportunities for work for the neighboring populations, most of whom lived in very poor, undeveloped, and rather inhospitable regions and were eager to move to the city. The majority of those who came to Dubrovnik worked in jobs which did not require particular skills and which were connected with Dubrovnik's prospering economy; some, however, came as merchants. The influx of Slavs only continued a migration which probably had begun in the tenth century and which was the main factor in the slavicization of Dubrovnik. By the thirteenth century, the continuing immigration of Slavs from the Balkan regions and from Dalmatia had stabilized the ethnic structure of Dubrovnik (see Chapter V).

The internal development of Dubrovnik in the first half of the fourteenth century was marked by an event of great importance. A number of the richest, most distinguished, and politically most influential families, whose members had for a long time exercised a leading role in the politics and economy of the city, closed their ranks and took exclusive political power into their hands, sharing it, of course, with the Venetian count as long as he was in Dubrovnik. This emergence of the Ragusan patriciate as a separate social group, and the only politically active one, took place very soon after the year 1332. From that time until the downfall of the Republic of Dubrovnik in 1808, this same group of families maintained complete political control for themselves.

The patricians began to emphasize their alleged Roman origins and character, and this attitude had social significance. By stressing their Romanism, the patricians tried to erect an additional barricade between themselves and the rest of the population, which, as we saw, was thoroughly slavicized by this time. However, the Ragusans—whether patricians or common people—did not have any interest in nationalistic distinctions between Croatians, Serbians, or other Slavic ethnic groups in the city. The patricians and citizens of Dubrovnik called themselves only *Raguseus* and *Ragusei*, or *Dubrovčani* in Slavic, which they felt was the most important and, in fact, the only possible denomination they could use for themselves.

The number of patrician families is not easy to determine. It has been shown recently that seventy-eight such families can be counted for the period up to the end of the fourteenth century, but a number of these families were already extinguished in the fourteenth century. Toward the middle of the fifteenth century, there were thirty-three patrician families in Dubrovnik. The figures on individual patricians are even more approximate, and only male adult members of the group were counted. It is now assumed that about the year 1312 there were around three hundred such men in Dubrovnik. In 1423 there were 391 male adult patricians; in the year 1427 there were 414; and in 1442, 553. This shows a considerable and rapid increase in the fifteenth century, but this pace of growth did not last long.

It is very hazardous to try to determine the ratio between this group and the rest of the population, because there are as yet no studies on the non-noble population of Dubrovnik. However, if for every male adult patrician at least another person is counted, then there were around 1,100 members of patrician families by the middle of the fifteenth century, which was certainly a high proportion of the whole popula-

33

tion of the city. There were always about ten families which represented the real core of patrician power and wealth and wielded the greatest influence in the city. Some of the families in this group—Menčetić, Sorkočević, Djurdjević, Gučetić, and Gundulić, for example—managed to preserve their position and influence for hundreds of years.

It is very important to stress that the Ragusan patriciate—like the Venetian—was not a feudal nobility in the Western European sense. Although it was eager to obtain land, it was not, properly speaking, a landed nobility. There was very little land, mostly poor, around Dubrovnik, and in the period before 1400 it was still in Serbian or Bosnian hands. When the Republic of Dubrovnik expanded and obtained some land, it gave the major portion to the patricians, but the land was never sufficient to support them economically. In addition to the patriciate, the church owned land, and only a small portion belonged to citizens and peasants. Interestingly enough, the ground inside the city itself was not state property but belonged exclusively to the patricians and the church.

Because the territory around Dubrovnik was of poor quality, even the biggest landowners, the patricians, had to turn elsewhere for the means to ensure a decent living for themselves and their families. This, of course, they found in trade—particularly the lucrative trade with the Balkan hinterland—in navigation, in credit and banking operations, in investments into crafts. In 1440, Philippus de Diversis, the Italian principal of the Ragusan high school, wrote in his *The Site of the Buildings, Policies, and Praiseworthy Habits of the Illustrious City of Ragusium*: "I call the nobles the supreme merchants, although some of them live only from incomes [from estates], but those are few." He added: "Some-one may wonder, why do I call nobles merchants, since nobility contradicts commerce. Let him know that the terri-tory of Ragusium, because of its sterility as much as because of the large number of people, lives off small income, so that nobody could live with his family from his possessions unless he had other riches, and this is why it is necessary to engage in commerce."

Thus the chief economic interest of the patriciate coincided with that of the common citizens. This facilitated their col-laboration. Furthermore, the richest families of the citizenry had created very early their own special group—the Fra-ternity of Saint Anthony, or *Antunini*—some of whom were as wealthy or wealthier than the patricians, though without political power. This had split the non-noble population and thus made it easier for the patricians to dominate. On the other hand, the patriciate, because of its own economic interests, furthered a policy which was in accordance with the interests of the merchants, captains, craftsmen, and others. Therefore, although there were minor dissatisfactions and anti-patrician feelings both in Dubrovnik and in its territor-ies, no major rebellion ever resulted.

While the patricians were the most important and power-ful group in Dubrovnik, the peasants were the most numer-ous. The status of the peasants differed in various times and in various parts of Ragusan territory. In the oldest portion, Astarea, estates apparently were cultivated mainly by slave manpower in early times, but by the thirteenth century the slave system had disappeared. The part of the estate that the landowner kept for himself was cultivated by laborers who worked for a salary and were free. Another part of the estate was leased by the landowner to peasants, who were obliged to give him part of their crops, usually half, and also to perform various other duties. This system was similar to the one prevailing in Dalmatia and in many Italian cities.

After the middle of the fourteenth century, however, when the bubonic plague struck hard at Dubrovnik, as it had throughout Europe, the Ragusan patriciate started enforcing measures which were meant to tie the peasants to their estates, because of the lack of manpower. This was a development leading toward serfdom, although serfdom itself never fully prevailed on Ragusan land. The peasants remained free; the landlords had no jurisdiction over them; the peasants' obligations were limited and established through a contract with the landlord; and the peasants were not bound to the land they cultivated. Nevertheless, there is no doubt that the patricians did work in many ways toward limiting the peasants' freedom. The obstacle to this goal of the aristocracy was the booming city of Dubrovnik and its constant need for manpower, which offered the peasants many possibilities to escape the hard conditions on the estates. Indeed, a number of peasants, sometimes with their landlord's blessing, became part of the city's life. It should be added that there were free peasants who had their own small lots of land in Ragusan territory, but their number was insignificant. The conditions of the peasants in territories gradually obtained by Dubrovnik from Serbians and Bosnians varied somewhat from those prevailing on Ragusan lands, but the new acquisitions were integrated rather quickly into the Ragusan system.

Like other medieval cities, Dubrovnik used slave manpower and traded in slaves, who came mainly from the Balkans until the end of the thirteenth century. The fact that many people in Bosnia were considered to be heretical Patarenes and others, both in Bosnia and in Serbia, were of the Orthodox faith served as an excuse to Ragusan merchants for using them as slaves. The Patarenes were not considered Christians, and members of the Orthodox Church were schismatics. Although slaves were used by the Ragusans on their estates in earlier times, more often they worked in homes in the city.

There was considerable trade in slaves from the Balkans through Dubrovnik toward Italy and other parts of the Mediterranean, including even the remnants of the Crusaders' state in Palestine before 1291. In the fourteenth century, accounts of Bosnian slaves disappeared almost completely from Ragusan records. This was probably because Ragusans started to hire increasing numbers of free men from surrounding lands, particularly as servants in their homes and shops. On the other hand, there was an increase in the importing of slaves from faraway regions—the Black Sea coasts, Asia Minor, Africa, and others—but this trade seems to have been less for Dubrovnik's own needs than for re-exportation toward Italy and the West.

On January 27, 1416, the Major Council, with seventy-five votes in favor and only three against, carried a motion which was of great importance to the future of slavery in Dubrovnik. Because neighboring lords constantly were complaining against Ragusan merchants, who were buying and selling their subjects, and "considering such a trade to be ugly, nefarious, and abominable and against all humanity, and

that it constitutes not a small burden and infamy to our city,
that is, that the human species, made to the image and
similarity of our creator, should be converted to merchandise
and be sold as if they were brute animals," the Major Council
decided that Ragusans and foreigners living in Dubrovnik
no longer could engage in any way in slave trade in the
territory from Budva in the south to Split in the north. However, "if a citizen or inhabitant of Dubrovnik bought a male
or female slave for his own usage," he would not be punished
in the way this decision established for other infractors. No
foreigner was to be allowed to engage in this kind of trade
in Dubrovnik, and no Ragusan ship was to be allowed to
carry slaves. The decisions of 1416 were in part reinforced by
additional orders in 1418 against violent or fraudulent ab-
duction of persons into slavery. The decision of 1416 has
frequently been presented as the abolition of slavery in Dubrovnik. It was certainly an important step in that direction,
and Dubrovnik must be given credit for being among the
first European cities to take such a measure. Nevertheless, it
was clearly a limited prohibition and left ample opportunity
for the institution of slavery to continue in the city (see
Chapter VI).

The closing of the ranks of the Ragusan patriciate after
1332 stabilized the structure and the role of the three governmental councils, which had been formed in the thirteenth
century. The *Consilium Maius*, the *Consilium Minus*, and
the *Consilium Rogatorum*, or Senate, now divided, more or
less clearly, their respective functions. The Major Council,
consisting of all adult male patricians over twenty years of
age (later, over eighteen), was the body which made the

most important general decisions concerning the political life of Dubrovnik and which also elected all important officials of the state. However, a large body like the Major Council could not meet frequently, and so the Minor Council took the role of executive body. It consisted of the head of state (*comes*, or count, before 1358, rector after that date) and ten councilmen. But it was the Senate which allocated to itself the leading role in the formulation and the main control of the execution of Ragusan political decisions. The Senate, consisting of thirty to forty prominent patricians, was, beyond doubt, the most important of the three councils from the point of view of both Dubrovnik's international politics and life inside the city itself.

It is worth noting that the governmental councils of the Ragusan state functioned on the basis of what could be called patrician democracy. The discussions were completely unrestricted. Everybody was free to speak out; then a secret ballot was taken. There always had to be two propositions on which to vote, if nothing else a "yes" and a "no" proposition. The vote was equal for all members of the councils, and the decisions were generally taken by simple majority. Once a decision was made, everybody was expected to obey it and act accordingly, even those who had voted against it. By the same token, those patricians or citizens who were entrusted by the councils with a diplomatic or other mission were expected to carry it out, regardless of the dangers and personal hardships. If a matter under discussion in a council was of special importance to the security of the state, it would be declared secret and nobody was allowed, under severe penalties, to divulge any information from the council meeting. Later these secret decisions were recorded in separate books, but unfortunately, because of their delicate nature, these volumes were frequently destroyed by the government.

The middle of the fourteenth century witnessed great changes in the whole eastern coast of the Adriatic. From the time Louis I took over as king of Hungary and Croatia in 1342, he waged war against Venice for the Dalmatian coast. This war was brought to an end by the Zadar Peace Treaty of February, 1358. The powerful Hungarian king, at the time one of the most important rulers in Europe, obtained a great victory. The Zadar Treaty gave him Dalmatia and Dubrovnik. Venice suffered a heavy defeat and a terrible loss. The region it had struggled to dominate since the year 1000 and over which it had managed to impose its rule after the Fourth Crusade was now lost. The doge was even obliged to give up his title of "*Dux Dalmatiae et Croatiae*." But the worst part was that a strong enemy had established itself in a region very close to Venice and there was a possibility that the two coasts of the Adriatic could fall under a single ruler. Louis was an Angevin and so were the rulers of southern Italy since the second half of the thirteenth century. The worst Venetian nightmares must have been haunting them after the Zadar Treaty, and with good reason.

The change of 1358 did not affect all the cities of the eastern Adriatic coast in the same way. Those of central and northern Dalmatia were more or less directly annexed to Hungary and subordinated to the king and to the ban of Croatia. This was an extremely important moment in Ragusan history. The city could either preserve the degree of independence it had, even increase it, or it could lose it and suffer a fate similar to that of the Dalmatian cities. Dubrovnik was fortunate enough to retain its independence. This was due in part to the fact that Dubrovnik's position under Venetian domination already was special and different from other cities. Also, its location was far removed from Hungarian power centers and there were no Hungarian armies nearby. Most important was the ability of Ragusan statesmen and diplomats, who in this fateful hour showed wisdom, maturity, restraint, and skill in their actions in the city itself and even more in their dealings with Hungary, Venice, and the other powers involved.

The result was the almost complete independence of Dubrovnik, as stipulated in the Treaty of Višegrad between Dubrovnik and Hungary in May, 1358. It is true that the city recognized the supreme authority and protection of King Louis of Hungary and Croatia and his successors, but this was only a formality. There was no Hungarian army or fleet in Dubrovnik. The degree of the city's independence can be seen best in the fact that the Ragusan's successfully resisted the attempt by Louis, immediately after the peace of Zadar, to impose his man as count in Dubrovnik, as the Venetians had done. From this time, the Ragusan patriciate started electing one of its own men to the position of rector of the city, but only for one month at a time and with strict limitations for re-election, to avoid any tendency toward dictatorship.

The recognition of the Hungarian protectorate consisted of a yearly tribute paid to the king and of prayers said for him in Ragusan churches on certain occasions. The king, in turn, offered protection to Dubrovnik, particularly in the diplomatic field. Dubrovnik communicated directly with the king, with the noblemen in his court, and with the ban of Croatia, either a Croatian or a Hungarian nobleman. But the Ragusan patriciate was completely free to guide its state the way it thought best and to shape its international policies according to its own evaluation of events and situations. This freedom of decision went so far that, through treaties with the Hungarian king, Dubrovnik was entitled to carry on commerce and to have normal relations with Serbia and Venice even if the king waged a war against them.

Dubrovnik was now freed from the limitations imposed by the Venetians on its navigation. Contrary to earlier opinions, we know today that this did not bring about a sudden and big swing in Ragusan trade and investments toward the sea. The hinterland trade remained by far predominant, but the abolition of Venetian-imposed barriers no doubt opened up new possibilities. One such opportunity came in 1373, when the Ragusans obtained from the pope a limited permit for trade with the "infidels" in Egypt and Syria. Some Ragusans had been going into those regions already in the thirteenth century, but this was a dangerous enterprise because of the papal prohibition of trade with the Moslems after the downfall of the Crusaders' state in Palestine in 1291. In its efforts to obtain this permit from the pope, Dubrovnik had the diplomatic support of its overlord, the king of Hungary. Obtaining the papal permit, with all its limitations, was a considerable success for Ragusan merchants because of the richness of the overseas market and the high value of goods which could be imported from there. It was also proof of the greatly increased Ragusan capacity to navigate to faraway lands, a fact further confirmed by the many permits obtained by individual Ragusan merchants from the papal chancellery during the 1370's and 1380's for navigation to "infidel" lands.

It is important to emphasize the coincidence of this new opening of Dubrovnik toward the sea with the beginning of troubles in the Balkan peninsula. The situation in that area began to decay rapidly for two main reasons: the premature and sudden death of the Serbian emperor, Stephen Dušan, in 1355 and the beginning of the penetration of the Ottoman Turks into Europe. Under Dušan, Serbia had attained the peak of its medieval development, and he was the first European ruler to grasp all the significance and the danger in the appearance of the Ottomans on European soil. Dušan tried to convince the pope, Venice, and other Western powers to organize an expedition under his command against the Ottomans. At a time when the Ottomans were only entering Europe and were present on a very small scale, Dušan's plan had a good chance of success. But he found no response in the West, and his sudden death caused the collapse of his plans before they could be put into operation.

The Ottoman danger in the Balkan peninsula started toward the middle of the fourteenth century. During the civil war in Byzantium between John V Palaeologus and John VI Cantacuzenus—a war in which Dušan intervened—the Ottomans started crossing the straits into Europe as auxiliary troops of the belligerents. Thus in a way the Europeans themselves contributed to their later doom, for the Ottomans soon crossed into Europe on their own account. Profiting by the disarray caused by an earthquake, they conquered the city of Gallipoli, on the Dardanelles, in 1354. By 1362 they had probably conquered the big and important inland city of Hadrianople and established their capital there, entrenching themselves firmly on European soil.

In Serbia itself things were going from bad to worse. Dušan's young son, Emperor Stephen Uroš (1355–71), lacked his father's ability, energy, and prestige and was unable to govern the enormous state he inherited. The powerful feudal lords, whom Dušan had kept under control, were now free to dominate the countryside, becoming more or less independent masters of various regions and frequently fighting among themselves and with their foreign neighbors. The Ragusan government was well aware of this situation, and in April, 1371, explained in a letter that the dissensions existing among Serbian barons were hindering the enterprises which Ragusan merchants had undertaken in Serbia previously and the Ragusans therefore were turning toward the sea.

Uroš did try to find a remedy to this situation. In 1365 he joined to his throne, as king, a distinguished nobleman and lord of a vast region in Macedonia, Vukašin Mrnjavčević, but to little avail. In 1371, Vukašin and his brother Uglješa, the despot of the region of Serres, met the Ottoman army near Černomen at the Maritsa River. In the battle which ensued, the Serbian army was completely defeated and both Mrnjavčević brothers were killed. This was the decisive moment of the Ottoman penetration into the Balkans. Their triumph over the Serbians opened wide the gates of the Balkan peninsula to their invasion, and it is possible to say that the Ottomans, after Maritsa, were never stopped until they reached Vienna two hundred years later.

To make things worse, in the same year, 1371, Emperor Uroš died without an heir, and the feudal, centrifugal forces were further strengthened. A second big battle against the Ottomans in 1389 on the Kosovo Plain resulted in a second Ottoman triumph. The most prestigious Serbian leader, Prince Lazar Hrebeljanović, was killed and the Serbian army was annihilated. Europe finally started realizing how dangerous the Ottomans were, and the Hungarians especially felt the danger approaching their own territories. Consequently, an expedition was organized and, led by the Hungarian king, Sigismund of Luxembourg, pushed its way toward the southeast along the Danube. It was eventually met by the Ottoman army near Nicopolis and utterly defeated in 1396. Sigismund himself, barely escaping death or captivity, returned to his lands via Constantinople and on his way visited Dubrovnik, where he was received with greatest respect.

Thus, in the second half of the fourteenth century, the main Ragusan trading area and source of income, Serbia, was torn by internal difficulties and exposed to external dangers. One of the results was direct conflicts between Dubrovnik and some of the newly independent Serbian feudal lords—for example, the conflict with Vojislav Vojinović in 1361–62 and another with Nikola Altomanović in 1370–71. All of this, however, did not prevent the Ragusans from going into Serbia. The mines at Rudnik, Novo Brdo, Trepča, Janjevo, and Kratovo, for example, were increasingly attractive with their wealth of silver, copper, iron, lead, and other minerals. At the same time, Serbian towns started developing at a faster pace, such as Prizren, Priština, Skoplje, and Belgrade, and later Smederevo and others. The Ragusans, already firmly entrenched in Serbia, could not take the risk of losing this important market by withdrawing in the face of an unstable situation which had affected their business very little.

At the same time, the Ragusan merchants strengthened their contacts with Bosnia, which in the second half of the fourteenth century was attaining its greatest political and economic importance. Under the rule of the ban and, from 1377, king, Tvrtko I (1353–91), Bosnia expanded to include vast Serbian and Croatian territories. Dubrovnik itself was completely surrounded by Bosnia on its land borders, and Tvrtko took over all the tributes the Ragusans previously paid to the Serbian rulers. Bosnia possessed by this time rich mines of silver, lead, and iron in such places as Srebrenica, Olovo, and Deževica, as well as the growing towns of Fojnica, Visoko, Kreševo, Jajce, and others. The increased opportunities, of course, attracted the Ragusans, who established their positions there as they had already done in Serbia.

It should be mentioned here that Dubrovnik, because of its reputation for political stability and economic progress, served as a repository for the treasures of many Serbian and Bosnian rulers and feudal lords and families. Emperor Stephen Dušan, King Vukašin Mrnjavčević, and his son Prince Marko, the famous hero of Yugoslav epic poetry, as well as many minor noblemen had their deposits in Dubrovnik. So did the Bosnians in the fifteenth century—the powerful Prince Sandalj Hranić, his nephew Herzog Stephen Vukčić-Kosača, and others—and the Serbian despot, George Branković.

The continuing trade with the Balkan hinterland called for

expanding maritime trade too. But in this respect the second half of the fourteenth century was not always favorable to Dubrovnik. After 1358 the Venetians and the Ragusans rather quickly started accusing each other of violating agreements relating to the navigation of their men, goods, and ships. It is not surprising, therefore, that Dubrovnik joined the anti-Venetian coalition in 1378, a coalition in which Dubrovnik's protector, the king of Hungary, played a major role. This was during the time of a war which had begun in the Levant with the Veneto-Genoese conflict over the tiny Byzantine island of Tenedos, at the entrance of the Dardanelles strait, but which had very rapidly spread toward the West and included other powers, such as Hungary, Dubrovnik, and northeastern Italian cities. The Genoese, with Hungarian and Ragusan help, brought the war home to Venice, directly attacking the city of Saint Mark. Failing there, they concentrated on the conquest of the nearby town of Chioggia. The Ragusans helped their allies with two ships. However, when the battle of Chioggia ended in utter defeat for the Genoese, the Ragusans managed to preserve their ships and to return to normalcy in their relations with Venice after the Peace of Turin in 1381.

The last two decades of the fourteenth century saw a considerable upsurge in Ragusan maritime activity. Ragusan ships ventured in increasing numbers toward far-removed regions, such as Sicily, Greece, Egypt, Cyprus, Syria, Asia Minor, Constantinople, and the Black Sea area. However, at the beginning of the fifteenth century, this development of sea travel was threatened by events taking place near Dubrovnik itself. The situation in the Adriatic became tense because of the fierce rivalry between Sigismund of Luxembourg and Ladislas of Naples, the southern Italian Angevin, for the Hungarian and Croatian crowns and for the possession of Dalmatia. This was the culmination of a long struggle which had begun in 1382 after the death of King Louis I of Hungary and Croatia and in which the Croatian aristocracy was playing a major role. The defeat of King Sigismund at Nicopolis in 1396 by the Ottomans spurred on a new series of rebellions against his rule in Dalmatia and Croatia, as well as in Hungary. His opponents elected Ladislas of Naples as king.

Nevertheless, Sigismund retained considerable influence in Hungary, Croatia, and Dalmatia, and Dubrovnik was one of the cities which consistently remained faithful to him. This was not an easy thing for the Ragusans to do. Ladislas of Naples, with a strong navy, was just across the Adriatic, and the Ragusans had a vital interest in maintaining contacts with southern Italy. However, they decided that it would be to their greater advantage to support Sigismund, which they did. In the end their decision proved to be correct. Ladislas did come to Dalmatia personally in the summer of 1403 and took the crown in Zadar as king of Hungary and Croatia, but Sigismund, later in the same year, by a skillful maneuver managed to destroy the following of Ladislas and to deprive him of much of his power in those lands. Ladislas returned to Naples, retaining, nevertheless, his claims to the regions on the eastern shores of the Adriatic and leaving his representatives there. Sigismund, in spite of the problems that he would still have to face, had emerged victorious from this struggle for power in Hungary, Croatia, and Dalmatia.

This was not the only difficulty Dubrovnik had to face at this time. From 1403 to 1405 the city was at war with the Bosnian kingdom, and Ragusan territories suffered heavy damages from Bosnian troops. Peace was eventually made, but a new and much more dangerous situation arose. King Ladislas of Naples, despairing, with good reason, of ever achieving his goals and pretentions on the eastern Adriatic coast, sold his rights to Dalmatia to the Venetians for 100,000 ducats in July, 1409. What Ladislas really had was very little: Zadar, Vrana, Novigrad, and the island of Pag. But the important thing was that Venice managed by this arrangement to establish a legal pretext for its reconquest of Dalmatia, and the Venetians did not hesitate in expanding their rule in the region. By 1420 the bulk of the Croatian islands and cities of Dalmatia—Rab, Pag, Brač, Hvar, Korčula, Zadar, Šibenik, Trogir, and Split, with Kotor in the south— became part of Venetian Dalmatia, remaining under Venetian rule until 1797, the end of the Venetian Republic.

The massive return of Venice into Dalmatia was decidedly a triumph for the city of Saint Mark. Its position was now stronger than it had ever been. Such a turn of events, of course, could not be viewed with enthusiasm by the Ragusans. On the contrary, they had every reason to fear for their own independence, with the powerful Venetians present in Dalmatia and on the Adriatic and their protector, Sigismund of Hungary, unable to do anything effective against Venice. It was Dubrovnik's own diplomatic skill and maneuvering which saved the city from suffering once again the fate of 1205 and enabled it to preserve its freedom.

While all of this was happening in the Adriatic area, in

the Levant there was real hope for the first time that the Ottomans might be thrown out of Europe. In 1402 they suffered a terrible defeat near Ankara at the hands of the Mongol army of Tamerlane, and a civil war lasting for ten years broke out in the Ottoman state. Unfortunately, the European powers were too preoccupied with their own internal problems and international conflicts to be able to exploit this situation in the East. It was only after 1440 that the West decided to try once again to crush the Turks. An expedition was organized, led by the king of Hungary and the great Hungarian general and statesman John Hunyadi. The Serbians also participated in the effort, and Venice, Dubrovnik, and other Western maritime states promised support. After initial successes in 1443, the Christian army suffered a crushing defeat near Varna in November, 1444, and this was the end of the last Western attempt to annihilate the Ottomans. It became evident to anybody with political knowledge of the Levant and the Balkans that the Ottomans were there to stay. The Ragusans were among those who realized the significance of this very early and, soon after Varna, started trying to find a *modus vivendi* with the new masters of the political scene in the Balkans.

Dubrovnik had every reason to do so. Throughout the first half of the fifteenth century, increasing numbers of Ragusans continued to go to Serbia and Bosnia, in spite of political instability and Ottoman invasions. Serbian mines were producing more silver than ever, and the Ragusans profited by this increased production through their roles as proprietors of mines, transporters of minerals, and so on. There also were Ragusan craftsmen in the Balkan hinterland and, more importantly, a considerable number of Ragusans, particularly patricians, in the service of the Serbian state. The majority of them held high positions in the court of the Serbian despots, in Serbian finance administration, and especially in Serbian diplomatic services. It must be stressed, however, that no matter how high their position in Serbia (and this was true elsewhere and in other periods), the Ragusans always remained closely linked to their fatherland. They almost invariably agreed not only to defend Dubrovnik's interests whenever necessary but also to follow the orders of the Ragusan government concerning their own attitudes and activities.

The Ragusan merchants constituted colonies in Serbia and Bosnia. These colonies had *ad hoc* functionaries to deal with problems arising among Ragusans, while conflicts involving Ragusan merchants and native populations were solved by mixed institutions. The numbers of merchants in various colonies were quite substantial in the fifteenth century—from a few dozen to several hundred men in one place at a time. In their business dealings in Serbia and Bosnia the Ragusans employed all the modern Western commercial techniques of the time, such as companies (mainly of the *collegantia* type), bills of exchange, and other banking operations. In this way they certainly contributed to the introduction of progressive Western business methods in the Balkan hinterland. The importance of contacts between Dubrovnik and that region can be seen in a letter written by the Ragusan government in May, 1436: "All the goods of the city of Dubrovnik are in Bosnia, in Serbia, and largely in Turkey, Albania, and Romania (that is, Byzantium)," while in Dubrovnik itself there were every day "Bosnians, Serbians, Greeks, Albanians, and men of other nations in great numbers."

Unfortunately, all of this activity did not help the Balkan states much. Pressed from the south by the Ottomans, the Serbians had to rely increasingly on the Hungarians for support and this certainly helped prolong Serbia's independence for a while. Also, Ottoman internal strife at the beginning of the century and its consequences, together with Ottoman preoccupation with other areas, favored Serbia's survival. But two internal factors helped Serbia retain its independence. The mines—particularly at Novo Brdo, with its silver mixed with gold—were bringing enormous wealth to the Serbian rulers. Also, two of them, Despot Stephen Lazarević (1389, despot from 1402 to 1427) and Despot George Branković (1427–56), were men of exceptional ability who managed, at least temporarily, to stabilize and even improve the Serbian position. There is no doubt that the role of the Ragusans was very important. By serving as middlemen in the exportation of Serbian silver and other products to the West, they provided the leading source of cash to the Serbian rulers and thus contributed to the preservation of independence. But Serbian freedom, or what was left of it, was doomed to destruction.

An important change was made in the Ragusan political vocabulary at the beginning of the fifteenth century. The usual denomination, the Commune of Dubrovnik, was replaced by a new name, the Republic of Dubrovnik. This change was connected not only with the increased economic and political importance of the city but also with its terri-

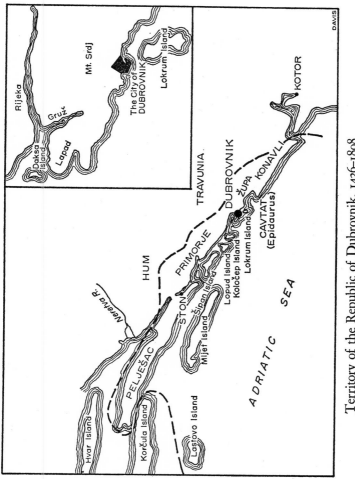

Territory of the Republic of Dubrovnik, 1426–1808

torial expansion. Indeed, it was in the first half of the fifteenth century that the Republic of Dubrovnik took its final territorial shape. From earliest times Dubrovnik possessed a narrow stretch of land called Astarea in the immediate vicinity of the city and the three small islands nearby: Koločep, Lopud, and Šipan. Toward the middle of the thirteenth century, the rather far-out island of Lastovo was added to Ragusan possessions. Later, in 1333—as previously mentioned— Dubrovnik bought the peninsula of Pelješac from the Serbians; in the 1360's it took possession of the important island of Mljet; and in 1399 the Ragusans obtained Primorje, the stretch of coast between Astarea and Pelješac, thus uniting their territories to the northwest. To the south, in 1419, Dubrovnik acquired part of the rich region of Konavli and in 1426, after a struggle with nearby Bosnian feudal lords, the second half of the area.

Thus Dubrovnik by 1426 had ended expansion of its territory, which encompassed approximately forty-five miles of land from northwest to southeast. Achieved mainly through peaceful means at the expense of Serbia and Bosnia, it was an expansion into agriculturally poor regions, except for Konavli. With the inclusion of Konavli, however, agriculture became somewhat more significant in the economy of Dubrovnik, though it never could match the importance of other activities. The Republic of Dubrovnik retained the territories obtained by 1426 without interruption until its disappearance in 1808. It is almost impossible to venture an estimate of population for these territories. It seems reasonable to assume, however, that the city of Dubrovnik itself, toward the end of the fifteenth century, had about 5,000 to 6,000 inhabitants, while the whole territory of the republic contained probably from 25,000 to 30,000 people.

In the 1430's Dubrovnik tried to obtain concessions for commerce in Morea but failed, and then suffered the same fate in attempting to obtain a privilege from the Byzantine emperor, John VIII, through the services of Ivan Stojković, one of Dubrovnik's illustrious sons at the time (see Chapter V). In 1433 the Ragusans did obtain an important concession from the ecclesiastical Council of Basle for navigation and trade in the lands of the "infidels." They also obtained privileges from the Byzantines only two years before the downfall of Constantinople; a Ragusan ambassador journeyed to Constantinople and to the Peloponnesus in 1451 and obtained charters with privileges from the last Byzantine emperor, Constantine XI, and from his brothers, Despots Thomas and Demetrius, in Morea. However, the advantages gained for the Ragusans were very short-lived.

Throughout the first half of the fifteenth century, Dubrovnik continued importing from the Balkans not only minerals but livestock, wax, wool, animal skins, furs, and some food as well. While the Ragusans kept part of these goods in their own city, they exported a much larger portion to the West and, in part, to the Levant. On the other hand, Dubrovnik was exporting to Serbia and Bosnia salt from Albania, from the island of Pag, and from the vicinity of Ston, and also textiles, mostly from Italy. In the fifteenth century, with the great increase in trade with the hinterland, Dubrovnik found it difficult to supply all the necessary textiles from Italy and decided to organize its own textile production. It was felt that this would liberate the Ragusan market from dependence on foreign, mainly Tuscan, merchants who were providing the city with most woven materials, not only from Italy, but also from Perpignan in France and from Flanders.

This is why, in the 1420's, Pietro Pantella, an Italian from Piacenza, was authorized and supported by the Ragusan government in developing the first large-scale textile production in Dubrovnik. His business expanded very rapidly and successfully, and he was soon joined by other Ragusan and foreign merchants and entrepreneurs, with the result that Dubrovnik became an important center for the weaving of fabrics (see Chapter VI). The new enterprise gave the city an additional, substantial economic boost. The need for raw materials sharply increased, particularly for wool, and Catalan merchants started bringing Spanish wool to Dubrovnik. A number of them settled in the city and played an important role in its life. At the same time, this activity attracted additional Slavic manpower from nearby lands to Dubrovnik, thus further strengthening the links between the city and the hinterland.

It should not be assumed, however, that crafts developed in Dubrovnik only at this time. There is mention of craftsmen and their activities in the earliest archival books found, those dating from the end of the thirteenth century. By the first half of the fifteenth century, craftsmen were organized into guilds named after the patron saints of the crafts. Throughout the fourteenth century there were increasing numbers of artisans, as well as a growing variety of crafts in Dubrovnik. Among the crafts were shipbuilding, masonry, carpentry, shoemaking, and tanning. There also were some more-specialized fraternities, for example, that for coral fishermen and one at least in which gold- and silversmiths were organized. All of them continued to develop and prosper in the fifteenth century, but some became particularly prominent—the fraternities of textile producers, shipbuilders, silversmiths, and painters, for example.

Large numbers of young men from the Balkan hinterland were constantly coming to Dubrovnik and working there with local artisans, thus gaining skills which some of them introduced in their native regions when they returned. However, most of the workers remained in Dubrovnik. At the same time, Ragusan craftsmen very frequently worked for Bosnian and Serbian rulers and feudal lords; sometimes they even went to Bosnia or Serbia to perform their jobs. This was, beyond any doubt, another way in which Dubrovnik acted very usefully as a link in the transmission of influences between East and West. In addition, with their increasing wealth, Balkan noblemen purchased many luxury items directly from Western artisans, particularly goldsmiths, either in Dubrovnik or with Ragusan intervention. For, in spite of two major conflicts with Bosnian potentates (Radoslav Pavlović in 1430–32 and the Herzegovinian duke, Stephen Vukčić-Kosača, in 1451–54), the contacts between Dubrovnik and the Balkan states continued uninterrupted until a complete change took place in the Balkan political situation.

This fateful change, was, of course, brought about once more by the Ottoman Turks. Sultan Mohammed II (1451–81), immediately upon taking over the government of his country, embarked on a policy of conquest. The Ottomans by this time had pushed as far north as the Danube, Bosnia, and Croatia, but they still had not eliminated the remnants of

Christian states behind them. Mohammed decided to take care of this before proceeding farther north, toward new conquests. By 1453 the Ottomans had taken Constantinople, thus abolishing the Byzantine (Eastern Roman) Empire after it had existed for 1,100 years. In 1459 the Ottomans did not have much trouble in conquering the last Serbian fortress, Smederevo, on the Danube, thus abolishing the Serbian medieval state. Next year they occupied the Peloponnesus, eliminating the last Byzantine despotates there, and at the same time also took the Greek Trebizond Empire in northern Asia Minor. In 1463 the Ottomans defeated the Bosnians, killed the last Bosnian king, and did away with the Bosnian medieval state. Two years later the conquerors occupied almost all of Herzegovina—a territory which had been a special political unit within the Bosnian kingdom since the first half of the fifteenth century—and became the direct neighbors of the Republic of Dubrovnik. In 1481 the sultan took the last remnants of Herzegovina, and finally, in 1499, the Ottomans conquered what was left of Zeta.

Thus, from the 1460's on, Dubrovnik was confronted with complete Ottoman domination in the Balkans, and the Turkish army was on Ragusan borders. Fortunately for the Ragusans, they had realized much earlier that this would happen and had established relations with the Ottomans. The first official political contacts began in 1392, with Ragusan attempts to negotiate with Sultan Bayazed I (1389–1402) guarantees for their commerce in the Balkans, which they managed to obtain in 1396. After that, contacts continued on and off, and the Ragusans intensified their search for a *modus vivendi* with the Ottomans after the Varna disaster in 1444.

In 1447 the Ragusans negotiated a treaty with the Turks which permitted them free commerce in the Balkans, but in 1458 a new and very important development took place. The Ottomans had insisted that the Ragusans pay them a yearly tribute, and Dubrovnik had tried to avoid this by all means, because paying this tribute could have placed the city in the position of an Ottoman vassal. However, after the downfall of Byzantium and in 1456 the death of the Serbian despot, George Branković, and with the will and ability of the new sultan clearly shown, Dubrovnik decided, with a heavy heart, to begin paying tribute to the Ottomans in 1458. At the time it consisted of a relatively small amount of money, only 1,500 ducats, and presents to the Turkish dignitaries, but during the next two decades the amount of the tribute grew steadily until finally, in 1481, it was fixed at 12,500 ducats a year. From then on, this tribute was paid annually to the Ottoman sultans. From the point of view of political reality, it can be said that the year 1481 marks the beginning of the Ottoman protection of Dubrovnik, although the protection of the king of Hungary and Croatia died out only after the battle of Mohács in 1526 in which the Ottomans defeated the Hungarian army and killed the king. With a brief interruption in 1684—when Dubrovnik had hoped for protection from the Austrians—the Ragusans remained faithful to their obligations toward the Ottomans until 1808.

The Ottomans allowed the Ragusans to carry on their activities in the conquered Balkan lands, and Dubrovnik

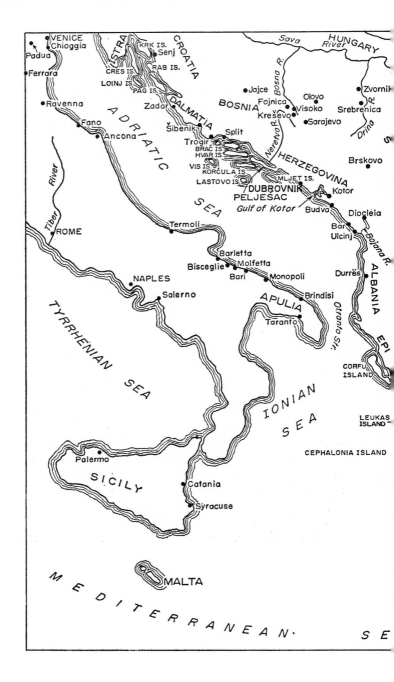

Dubrovnik's Trade Area

greatly benefited by such concessions (see Conclusion). At the same time, the city established excellent relations with the Aragonese kingdom in southern Italy in the second half of the fifteenth century; it was sympathetic to the efforts of Pope Pius II to organize a new crusade against the Turks, as well as to the brave struggle of George Kastriotes Scanderbeg in Albania and of the Hungarian and Croatian king, Matthias Corvinus, in the north, against the Ottomans. But the Ragusans were experienced statesmen and political realists, and they knew that all these efforts were too few and too small to make any fundamental change in the situation in the Balkans. They were firmly convinced that, by preserving their position in the Balkans through their arrangements with the Ottomans, they were doing the only reasonable and positive thing that could be done under the circumstances. And, indeed, by managing to keep the role of middleman between the Balkans and the West, even under Turkish domination, Dubrovnik continued to prosper and to make a valuable contribution to European development as a whole.

III

The Building of the City

VISITORS to Dubrovnik, both yesterday and today, have found it to be one of the most beautiful cities in the world. A special combination of natural setting and human endeavor has little by little created the city that exists today, with its magnificent walls, its monumental churches, its elegant palaces, and its peculiar, unique vistas. The city was shaped through hundreds of years of extraordinary human efforts, accompanied by natural phenomena, primarily earthquakes, which often changed human projects and destroyed human achievements. As much as the natural setting of Dubrovnik has been one of its great assets, it also has been one of its great handicaps throughout history.

When the refugees from Epidaurus settled on the high rock above the sea in the seventh century, they were, in fact, on a small island separated from the mainland by a shallow sea channel. On the other side of the channel there was the slope of the mountain Srdj, rising from sea level up to about 1,400 feet. Because of the proximity of Slavs, it is not surprising that the refugees wanted to fortify their position on the rock as soon as they could. Unfortunately, for the whole period before the archival documents begin—that is, until the 1270's—there is little information, other than that from local chroniclers and analysts, about how the city was built and fortified. Still, by combining that information with a few facts given by Constantine Porphyrogenetus and taking into consideration the situation of the new settlement at the time, it is possible to obtain an approximate picture of the development of the city.

The settlers on the high rock did not have to worry much about the southern side facing the sea. The incline was so steep that there was no danger of anybody attacking the new city from the sea. The northern side, toward the mountain, presented a different problem. Although the sea channel separating the island from Srdj Mountain provided a degree of security from the Slavs, it was not sufficient, because the rock had a lesser slope on this side. Therefore, for defense from possible Slavic attacks, the first fortifications were built. The earliest fortress, called Castellum, was built on the highest portion of the rock, probably in the first half of the seventh century. It was constructed of stacked stone and wood. Nothing remains of it except the name of a former monastery, Sancta Maria de Castello, which probably was erected later on the same spot. That whole part, the oldest *sexterium* of the city, was called Castellum until the beginning of the nineteenth century.

Another *sexterium*, Saint Peter, was added to the south of Castellum, and the two were surrounded by a second wall, also built of stacked stone and wood. A later city wall of stone and lime, probably built at the end of the eighth century, replaced this one. On the southern side, along the sea, the walls ran east, high on top of the rock, approximately the way they do today; then they turned northward, excluding the later Pustijerna *sexterium* to the east. The strongest part of the wall was, not surprisingly, the northern one, facing the mainland, where there were several gates and towers. The western side of the wall included the westernmost part of the rock, overlooking the small bay to the west, as it does at present. There was considerable space left between the city inside the wall and the channel to the north, because that area was flat and inconvenient for fortifications.

The second extension of these early walls came when the Pustijerna quarter—easier to fortify—was enclosed within them, though the exact date of this inclusion is not known. Pustijerna was not as high and steep as the first portion of the city, but it was rocky and, if wisely fortified, could become a formidable extension of the expanding Ragusium. The city needed to expand, because, as we have seen, its population, together with its navy and activity in general, was increasing. Constantine Porphyrogenetus and several local chroniclers described how the Arabs attacked Ragusium in 866-67 and, after fifteen months of unsuccessful siege, were forced to withdraw upon arrival of the Byzantine fleet. It seems justified to assume that the city at that time already had strong walls and not so small a population. Constantine Porphyrogenetus also says that the Ragusans had built first a small city, then a bigger one, and then they had enlarged the walls, so as to obtain a city, which enabled them to expand and to multiply. All of this seems to indicate that the three *sexteria* of Ragusium, those on the rocky, southern side, were surrounded by the walls before the middle of the ninth century.

It is almost certain that from very early times there was a bridge crossing the channel from the mainland to the island on which Ragusium was built. This bridge spanned the western side of the channel where it was narrowest, near the present western entrance to the city. Near the bridge on the mainland side was a large, strong tower, built by the Ragusans in 972, according to all local chroniclers. Its purpose was to control access to the bridge. On the other side, on the island, stood the first Church of Saint Blaise. The tower existed until the nineteenth century, when it was destroyed by the Austrians. Constantine Porphyrogenetus mentions the Church of Saint Stephen "in the middle" of Ragusium. The remnants of this church still can be seen, and they are in Pustijerna, which means that by the middle of the tenth century that part of Ragusium was completely integrated with the remaining two parts inside the walls. The only visible difference was that the little, narrow streets of the two other *sexteria* had taken winding patterns, shaped by the environment, and the streets in Pustijerna were straight, built according to a plan.

The eleventh century, as we have seen, was a very important period in the development of Ragusium, and it seems that at this time the inhabitants first moved out of their bastioned city on the rock and established a new fortification which was not part of the existing defensive system. This new fortification was built on a steep, high rock west of the city itself. Its position was of great strategic importance. It

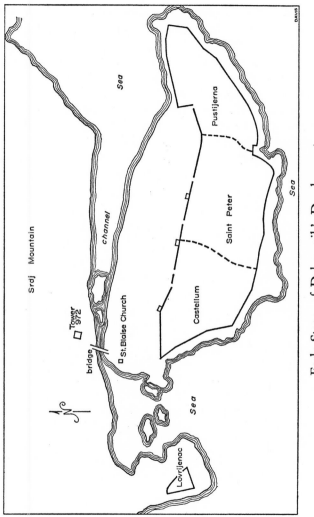

Early Stages of Dubrovnik's Development

dominated western access to the island and the city of Ragusium; it was well situated to control movement on the sea; and it was almost at the same height as the western walls of Ragusium itself, but separated from them by a small bay. The new fortress came to be known as Lovrijenac, "the fort of Saint Lawrence," because of the small church of the saint built inside it. There is no secure proof that this stronghold was begun in the eleventh century, but the local chroniclers were unanimous in attributing it to that period, which seems reasonable, considering the situation in the region as a whole. Of course, the original fortress certainly was a far cry from the imposing, majestic structure, towering high above the sea, that exists today.

During the twelfth century, Ragusium grew and developed, and Slavs were increasingly drawn into the city, many of them probably settling in the suburb, or *burgus*, on the flat stretch of land between the walls and the channel. It seems plausible to agree with the conclusion of recent research that, by the first half of the thirteenth century, the city had crossed the channel and expanded northward and that new walls of stone and lime were being built to defend the new parts of Dubrovnik. However, it was only in the second part of that century that new *sexteria* were organized and that the channel was filled in and made into the main thoroughfare, or Placa, of the expanded city. The three new *sexteria* in the recently walled territory were those of Saint Blaise, Saint Mary, and Saint Nicholas. It is noteworthy that, with these additions, five out of six of the *sexteria* were on the southern side of the ancient channel, now Placa, while only one, Saint

Nicholas, encompassed the whole of the expansion to the north of Placa, on the mountain slope.

The new walls, of course, were not built at once, and sometimes there were difficulties in the process. In 1282 it was reported to the count and the justice court of Dubrovnik that two towers belonging to Martol Crijević had been built "on the wall of the Commune of Ragusium." Lest the commune should lose its rights, the court ordered Crijević either to come to terms with the government or to tear down the towers. Crijević contended "that the towers were built publicly and openly and also were for the defense of the city at a time when the new city wall had not been made, and so it is not to be believed that the said towers were built without knowledge and agreement of the Commune of Ragusium, but it is rather to be believed that they were made with the agreement of the commune and that the commune gave of its own to build the same towers for the fortification and protection of the city; also, Martol's grandfather and father owned the said towers in ancient times without question." Therefore, Crijević asked that he be freed of all charges, and the court, having examined the case and taken the oath from "several old and honest men," dismissed the charges.

It took about thirty years in the second half of the thirteenth century to complete the new walls of Dubrovnik. Strong and ingeniously built, they were able not only to withstand enemy attacks but also to deprive the enemy of the possibility to creep up unseen. Only parts of these ramparts survive today, but the plan was almost identical with the walls as they exist today, except for the eastern portion.

Within the enclosure, new parts of the city had to be built.

The planning and the decisions concerning this important activity were the responsibility of the government. In the Ragusan statute of 1272 there are a number of decisions concerning street planning. The interesting thing is that the new streets were laid out in straight lines throughout the new parts of the city, and winding thoroughfares remained only in the oldest parts of the city. In fact, straight streets have remained one of the characteristics of Dubrovnik, for the thirteenth-century street plan is essentially the same as that existing today.

The new center became Placa, formerly the channel, now the largest street in town. The other streets were planned so they would flow toward Placa from the southern and the northern sides and join the main street at a right angle; a few stretched east and west, parallel to Placa. The vast majority of streets were narrow. The statute of 1272 ordered those running north and south to be about 7.5 feet wide, while the 1296 additions to the statute put their width at about 8.5 feet. This, of course, meant that the houses in the city, particularly at their lower levels, were rather dark. A differentiation must be made, however, between the dwellings in the old part of the city and those constructed in the new sections. In the old part, on the rock, there was a great number of houses built over vaults above the streets. This gained additional housing space but deprived the streets and the basements of light and air. In the new part of the city this pattern of building was almost nonexistent.

Another important thing to note is that the layout of streets in the new part of the city facilitated the circulation of air. Generally speaking, the climate in Dubrovnik is very mild; the cold winds from the mountains of the hinterland are weak and rare, while the prevailing winds are those from the sea, particularly the southern wind, or sirocco. This wind often brings rain, and there is much humid and rainy weather from autumn till spring, but the temperature stays relatively high, and in every season there is much sunshine. The straight streets and the large central space of Placa certainly played an important role in easing living conditions during the humid winter season and in providing some relief during the hot summer days.

In the first half of the fourteenth century, with the city definitely united into one urban entity, the Ragusans proceeded to improve it further and to strengthen the walls and fortifications. They had good reason, in view of the Serbian hostility which lasted, with interruptions, until 1328. The improvement consisted mainly of building new towers. The first one was started in 1305 near the western wall, and it exists to this day under the name of Puncijela. The next was the fortress Minčeta on the northwestern corner of the walls, which was begun in 1319. Located in the highest spot of the city walls, this fortress later became, and is today, the crown of the whole system of walls around the city. However, in the first half of the fourteenth century, it was built only as a square tower, as were the others.

Throughout this half-century, not only were towers being built, but access to the fortifications and the organization of guard duty were improved. Besides the Puncijela and Minčeta towers, three others were built along the western wall of the city, while five were added to its northern side. On the eastern side, where the city harbor was located, the situation was somewhat more complicated. There it was a question not only of building fortifications but also of creating the best conditions under which ships could find shelter in the harbor from weather as well as from enemies. On the northern side of the harbor a tower, Saint Luke's, was built and, toward the middle of the fourteenth century, construction on still another, Saint John's, was begun on the southern side of the port, both of them existing today. An iron chain stretching between the two towers prevented access to the harbor by enemies. To break the onslaught of the waves, a dike of rocks was built on the far side of Saint John's tower. A number of measures also were taken to strengthen the walls on the sea side, but evidently this was the least menaced part of the fortifications and therefore the least cared for. On the whole, toward the middle of the fourteenth century, the city of Dubrovnik in its entirety was surrounded by a wall averaging five feet in thickness and was flanked by some thirteen tall, square towers. It is important to note that in 1345 a committee was created to take care of the fortifications and the protection of the city. This committee, consisting of patricians, became a permanent institution and lasted as long as the Republic of Dubrovnik itself.

A new era in warfare and consequently in the building of fortifications came with the introduction of firearms into Europe in the first half of the fourteenth century. In Dubrovnik this weaponry was mentioned in the second half of the century. The government was confronted with a serious problem: how to adapt and improve the existing fortifications and to build new ones to withstand attacks made with the use of firearms. In 1351 the Ragusans already had started building an additional outside wall (*antimuro*) on the western side, near the Pile gate, which eventually stretched along the whole western wall and later along the northern one as well. Its oblique structure improved considerably Dubrovnik's defense capability against firearms.

The events of 1358 introduced another disturbing element into Dubrovnik's defense planning. In that year the Venetians lost Dalmatia and Dubrovnik. Although the Dalmatian cities and coast were occupied by the Hungarians, Dubrovnik was able to preserve its independence under Hungarian protection. The new situation meant, however, that Dubrovnik might be confronted with its former masters, the Venetians, in a less than friendly way, and indeed this did happen rather soon. The Ragusans were aware of the danger and increased their efforts to improve their fortifications and the defense system as a whole. This became especially necessary in 1378, when Dubrovnik joined the anti-Venetian coalition and became involved in a major war in the Adriatic. The city walls on the sea side were improved and armed with a number of cannon; a moat was hastily dug outside the western wall; and measures were taken for the defense of the harbor. These efforts continued even after the war ended in 1381, particularly the long and difficult task of digging the moat (*Fossatum*, which gave the name Posat to a nearby part of Dubrovnik today).

Another significant change resulting from the events of 1358 was in the number of city gates in Dubrovnik. As soon as the last Venetian count left Dubrovnik, the government ordered all but four gates to the city to be walled in. Of the four left open in 1358, three survive and are still in use: the western gate (Pile), the eastern gate (Ploče), and the gate leading into the harbor (known as Ponta gate). A fourth gate left open at that time was walled in in 1612; however, in 1381 another gate, called the Fishmarket gate, was opened in the wall near the arsenal, and it exists to the present time. The four city gates remained the only entrances to the city until the nineteenth century, when the Austrians opened two more. As long as the Republic of Dubrovnik lasted, these four entrances to the city were carefully guarded by noblemen who commanded small troop detachments. The eastern and western gates were equipped with drawbridges, and somewhat later accesses to these drawbridges were built into stone bridges crossing part of the moat.

In addition to taking constant care of the city walls, the government of Dubrovnik had to find a way to use the arsenal safely. Organized in 1329 on a Venetian order, the arsenal occupied a central place in the harbor and was wide open toward the sea, while, at the same time, it was located close to the heart of the city, at the eastern end of Placa. The Ragusan government repeatedly took measures to ensure that no enemy could use this facility to penetrate into the city, and this never happened. Another cause of concern which, like the arsenal, was basically a result of the development of Dubrovnik and the increase of its importance was the defense system of the city of Ston, obtained in 1333 from the Serbian ruler, Stephen Dušan, with the peninsula of Pelješac. The Ragusans had little by little built an important network of fortifications there which stretched for about 2.7 miles and enclosed not only Ston but the whole isthmus of Pelješac. These fortifications exist to this day.

Throughout the first half of the fifteenth century, Dubrovnik's efforts to increase the efficiency of its walls continued
and were certainly stimulated by the growing Ottoman
menace. It is significant that the two fortresses which seem
to have received the most attention in this period were
Minčeta, the highest tower on the northwestern corner of
the walls and the one most exposed toward the mountain
Srdj, and Lovrijenac, the fortress separate from the walls,
perched high on the rock to the west of the city. But the
Ragusans also paid much attention to the improvement of
the walls of their city toward the sea and around the harbor.
The most important result of this was the building of the
tower of Saint Marguerite, located in a key position on the
southern wall. Finally, on the eastern side the walls were
extended to enclose the Dominican monastery which until
then had been outside the walls. Thus, by the middle of the
fifteenth century, the walls of Dubrovnik acquired their final
extent—about 6,470 feet—which they have preserved until
today, but their height, depth, and forms were still to be
improved to make them more efficacious and capable of
withstanding any possible enemy attack.

These improvements took place in the second half of the
fifteenth century and the first half of the sixteenth. The fall
of Constantinople in 1453, followed by the Ottoman conquest of the Balkan states, induced the Ragusans to increase
their efforts to fortify the city. In addition, the fortifications
were a good guarantee against any Venetian threat, the
possibility of which increased after the Venetian return into
Dalmatia at the beginning of the century. The works, of
course, were enormously expensive, for the walls were to

be from sixteen to twenty feet deep and about sixty-five feet high. It is sufficient to look at them as they stand today to imagine what a tremendous amount of money and manpower must have been invested in their building. The government had the power to recruit all the population inside and outside the city for the construction of these walls. The Ragusans did not shrink from spending the necessary sums or from putting people at hard work, for they knew that the walls, together with their shrewd diplomacy, were the only guarantee of their freedom. Both the walls and the diplomacy depended very much on, and were made possible by, the flourishing Ragusan trade of the time, particularly between the East and the West.

Among the architects who took part in the construction of the walls were local ones and also a number of foreigners. Thus in the fifteenth century we find the names of Beltramus from Milan, Franciscus Teutonicus from Germany, Bernardinus from Parma, and others. One man who worked very long and enjoyed great prestige in Dubrovnik was Onofrio de la Cava from southern Italy. He built other important objects in Dubrovnik but was engaged largely in the building of fortifications. Another even more noted architect was the famous Florentine Michelozzo Michelozzi. He, too, took part in other building activities but was prominent in the shaping of the Minčeta fortress. Although the idea to make this fortress circular had existed at least since 1455, Michelozzo, who worked in Dubrovnik from 1461 to 1463, gave it final form. However, he did not complete the project, and Minčeta was finished under the supervision of still another outstanding architect, Juraj Dalmatinac (George the Dalmatian), a Croatian from Dalmatia and builder of the magnificent cathedral in Šibenik. Michelozzo also drew up the plans for another important fortress on the western walls of the city—Bokar—which exists to this day, and he contributed considerably to the fortifications of the northern walls of the city. Mention must also be made of Paskoje Miličević, a prominent local architect in the late fifteenth and early sixteenth century, who for fifty years directed the building of Ragusan fortifications, as well as other works.

In the second half of the fifteenth century, the Ragusans, frightened by the Ottoman arrival at their border, increased the tempo of their defense measures. They did not hesitate to destroy buildings when they considered that step necessary for their security. This fate befell several small houses and chapels outside the city walls which were considered potential bulwarks for an attacker. In such cases the government ordered the destruction of the buildings with the understanding that the owners would be reimbursed or that new houses or churches would be constructed inside the city walls. On the other hand, the only fortress outside the walls, Lovrijenac, was the object of constant attention and improvement, and a proud inscription was engraved above the entrance to this majestic fortress: "*Non bene pro toto libertas venditur auro*," which translates, "Freedom is not sold for all the gold of this world."

The second half of the fifteenth century also witnessed two major developments in the growth of Dubrovnik. One was the enlargement and improvement of the city harbor and its fortifications—a logical consequence of expanding Ragusan navigation and maritime trade. However, because of the limited space available, it was a delicate task. This work, like all other works in the city and its walls, had to be approved by the government after the presentation of plans and, in some instances, wooden models of the new developments. The second important event was the beginning of construction on the Revelin fortress outside the eastern gate of the city. The work, which started in 1478, was only a modest beginning of the later mighty fortress. It is interesting to note a decision of the government to the effect that every day, in addition to nearby peasants, thirty families from Dubrovnik would be selected who would have to send their servants to work on the Revelin or pay a fine.

The major work on the Revelin started only in 1539, when Dubrovnik, frightened by the creation of the First Holy League of the pope, Venice, and Spain against Turkey, felt threatened by Venetian appetites and decided to fortify its eastern access. The commander of the Spanish fleet, the famous Genoese admiral Andrea Doria, sent to the Ragusans his engineer, Antonio Ferramolino, from Bergamo, and the new Revelin was built according to his plans. The urgency felt in Dubrovnik can be seen in the decision of the government to suspend all other public and private works in the city for four months and to put all masons, blacksmiths, and other workers at the disposal of the Revelin builders. Similar decisions were made in the following years, and by the middle of the century the fortress was more or less completed, becoming another strong, impressive building and standing unchanged to this day. With the completion of the Revelin, all the major fortifications of Dubrovnik assumed the positions

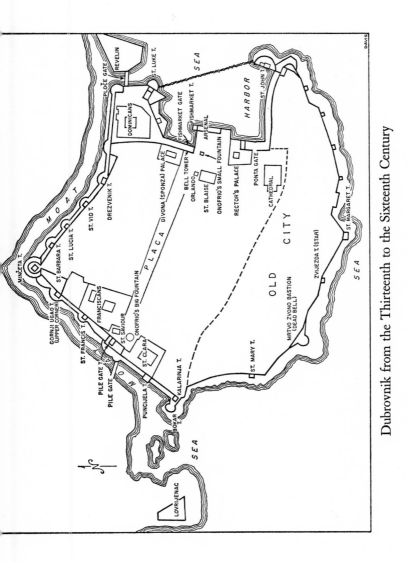

Dubrovnik from the Thirteenth to the Sixteenth Century

they occupy today. There were some minor additions and improvements after this period, but the basic work was done.

Inside the walls the city was developing at an increased rate, as shown in the construction of houses, palaces, and churches. In the second half of the thirteenth century, when Dubrovnik became one city through the union of the old urban parts on the rock with the predominantly Slavic suburbs near and across the channel, three types of houses were to be seen: those built of stone and lime, those built of stone and mud or stone and wooden beams (*maceria*), and those built solely of wood. Most houses in the oldest part of the city were built of stone and lime, while in the new parts wooden and *maceria* houses were most numerous. Because the majority of dwellings were wooden, it is not surprising that fires were a frequent occurrence. One such fire in 1296 destroyed almost the whole new part of the city. Afterward the government tried to induce the population to build stone and lime houses, but with limited success. Although wood was scarce in and around Dubrovnik and had to be brought in on ships, mainly from Albania and Croatia, and stone was plentiful everywhere near the city, the Ragusans continued long into the fourteenth century to build many wooden houses because they were cheaper. There were also *maceria* houses but in very small numbers, and by the beginning of the fifteenth century they had disappeared.

Repeated fires and growing prosperity, together with government pressures, convinced increasing numbers of Ragusans to switch to stone houses in the second half of the fourteenth century. But the decisive moment came in 1406 when still another fire swept away a number of wooden houses.

This induced the government to decree that all wooden houses must be destroyed and replaced by stone or *maceria* ones. A special committee was set up to evaluate all the wooden houses. Then each year a group of twenty-five houses was designated for destruction through the drawing of lots from a number of cards, each listing twenty-five dwellings. The houses had to be torn down within a year from the day they were designated. The owners were entitled to one-third of their value plus wood, tiles, iron, and other materials necessary to build new houses, except stone. The owners of wooden structures who wanted to tear down their houses and build stone ones before they had to were entitled to the same payment, but those whose dwelling places came up for rebuilding and who disobeyed the order would have their houses destroyed and would lose the advantages that the state was providing.

In this way, between 1406 and 1412, one hundred and seventy-five wooden houses were torn down, mainly in the lower part of the town and in the *sexterium* of Saint Nicholas. Besides these, a number of other wooden houses were voluntarily destroyed by their owners, and by 1413 there were only seventeen left in the whole city. The wooden houses were usually small structures, consisting of a ground floor and possibly a second floor above it, with one or two rooms all together. In early times they were roofed with straw, but from the end of the thirteenth century the government insisted that roofs be made of tiles. The value of these houses on the whole was low. The last seventeen of them, at the beginning of the fifteenth century, had a value of from twenty-one to 180 Ragusan hyperperi (that is, approximately

8.5 to 72 Venetian ducats), although some of the previously destroyed ones were evaluated at up to three hundred hyperperi (120 ducats).

Many Ragusans did not wait until 1406 to start building stone houses. In the old part of the city, as mentioned earlier, stone houses had prevailed for a long time, and by the first half of the fifteenth century they were spreading into the new parts of Dubrovnik, around Placa and to the north of it. Of course, the first to build such dwellings were the patricians. They were the most prestigious and also the richest people in town. Many of them had seen better houses and living conditions in Venice and other Italian cities, and they started emulating them. The patricians built their new homes almost exclusively of stone brought from the island of Korčula, located between Dubrovnik and Split and famed then, as now, for its excellent quality of stone. Particular care was paid to house doors and windows, which frequently were decorated and imitated the windows of Venetian houses. The stone houses might be as tall as four stories, and in the fifteenth century there even were houses with five floors. The fifteenth-century houses were not only bigger but also richer in ornamentation; their interior structure and decoration were much improved as well (see Chapter VI).

Of course, not all the dwellings in Dubrovnik became palaces at this or in later times. Many houses in which poor people and those in lower social classes lived were built without much planning and with complete disregard for appearance. Such were the majority of houses in narrow streets away from Placa and other central streets and squares. Three or four stories high, very narrow (sometimes only ten to fourteen feet wide), these houses frequently had only one room per floor, and, being poorly built, they were very hot in summer and cold in winter. Many of them, built mainly in the upper parts of the city, on rocks, are still standing and inhabited, while the majority of the patrician houses, built in the lower, central parts of the city, were destroyed in the terrible earthquake of 1667. In fact, the city as it is today— particularly Placa and its immediate vicinity—is much more the result of a hasty but harmonious post-earthquake reconstruction than the remnants of the original Dubrovnik of the fourteenth and fifteenth centuries.

Philippus de Diversis wrote in 1440 that in the city itself and in the surrounding areas there were many beautiful houses and palaces, looking as if the same man had built them. These buildings were not only beautiful but, according to de Diversis, also very luxurious and orderly, so that they would have been an asset to any Italian or Tuscan city. He added that many buildings both private and public in Dubrovnik were real embellishments for the city.

Among the public buildings, the one which most deserved designation as an adornment to the city was the Rector's Palace. Even today this palace is the most beautiful building in Dubrovnik. Its shaping lasted a long time and was marred by all sorts of difficulties. It seems that at the beginning of the thirteenth century, on the spot where the palace was later located, there was a fortification defending one of the gates to the old city. Once the city spread and the new walls were built, the seat of government was moved into a palace built near the tower, which was absorbed little by little into the new structure. The government was completely concentrated in this building, from the count (later rector) and the three councils, to the justice courts, the notaries, the chancellery, and even the jails. Also, arms and powder were stored in the old tower because they were too precious and delicate to be put away elsewhere. The result was that in 1435 a tremendous explosion blew up almost the whole of the Rector's Palace. The rebuilding was entrusted to the Italian architect, Onofrio de la Cava, who created a square structure with a central court, a ground floor, a mezzanine, and two additional floors. There was an ample loggia in the western façade, while at the four corners of the palace stood four square towers; a bell tower occupied the southern side.

In 1463, however, there was a second ammunition explosion. Although this one did not destroy the palace as the first one had, it did cause heavy damage. The building lost the second story, which was never rebuilt, and the angular towers were lowered to the level of the rest of the palace. There was an attempt made to build a completely new palace to replace the mutilated one, and Michelozzo Michelozzi was given the task of drawing up plans. The government, however, found his project too expensive and therefore had the existing palace repaired, with the result more or less as we see it today: a mixture of basically Gothic elements and Renaissance touches. The earthquake of 1667 damaged the building, but it was quickly restored. Even the famous inscription carved in stone above the entrance to the hall of the Major Council still stands: "*Obliti privatorum, publica curate*" which translates, "Having forgotten your private, take care of public affairs."

The second palace which today graces Dubrovnik's center

is the Divona or Sponza Palace. It was built by Paskoje Miličević in the second decade of the sixteenth century. Its rich façade contains an even greater mixture of Gothic and Renaissance elements than does the Rector's Palace. The ornaments were the work of the Andrijić brothers from the island of Korčula. Inside the Sponza Palace were the Ragusan mint, the customs house, and later the first Ragusan academy, where cultivated Ragusans and foreigners gathered together to discuss subjects of common interest.

In the process of Dubrovnik's formation as a city in the architectural sense, the churches and monasteries played a major role. The position and role of the church in Dubrovnik will be discussed later (see Chapter V). Here we are concerned only with its main building activities. There are four major ecclesiastical buildings of particular interest from the fourteenth and fifteenth centuries: the cathedral, the Church of Saint Blaise, the Franciscan monastery and church, and the Dominican monastery and church.

The cathedral, Saint Mary the Major, was started at the very end of the twelfth century, and its beginnings are connected with the English king Richard the Lion-Hearted. In fact, all the local chroniclers and analysts tell the story of Richard's ship being caught in a terrible storm on his return trip from Palestine in 1192, and the king making a vow to build a church to Saint Mary on the spot where he landed and another in England. Richard disembarked on the tiny island of Lokrum, off Dubrovnik, and wanted to build the church there. But the Ragusan government managed to persuade him to give the money for the building of a cathedral in the city itself, since on Lokrum a church and a monastery of the Benedictines already existed. It seems probable that the king gave a substantial amount of money to the Ragusans as a help toward building the cathedral, and this allowed them to start the work in 1199. The building continued throughout the thirteenth and the first half of the fourteenth centuries, and many local, Italian, and French architects took part in the construction. The result was a magnificent Romanesque church, in front of which in 1326 a beautiful baptistry was built from red and white marble. Unfortunately, neither of these buildings survived. The cathedral, richly ornamented on the inside as well as on the outside, was completely destroyed by the 1667 earthquake and a baroque church was built in its stead, while the baptistry was torn down by the Austrians in the nineteenth century.

It seems that the earliest protector saints of Dubrovnik were the typically Byzantine saints, Sergius and Bacchus, but sometime in the tenth century their cult apparently was abandoned and that of Saint Blaise, another Greek saint, was introduced. Statues of Saint Blaise can be seen to this day everywhere on the city walls and gates of Dubrovnik and in many other places. The first small church dedicated to him seems to have been built outside the earliest walls, near the little bridge which connected Ragusium, then still on an island, with the mainland. However, with the expansion of the city and the building of its new walls, the need arose for a bigger church in a better position. So a new Church of Saint Blaise was started in 1348 in a central location at the eastern end of Placa, not far from the government's palace and the cathedral. Actually, the cathedral and the Church of

Saint Blaise were being built partly at the same time, for the cathedral took a long time to finish. A mixture of Romanesque and Gothic styles gave the Church of Saint Blaise its particular charm. The earthquake of 1667 ruined only part of the church, but in 1706 it burned down completely and was rebuilt immediately in the rather unfitting baroque style.

The Franciscans first built their monastery outside the city walls, at Pile, but at the beginning of the fourteenth century, when the government of Dubrovnik was busy fortifying the walls and eliminating potential enemy bulwarks outside them, the Franciscans had to abandon their ancient site and build a new monastery inside the city. It was constructed close to the western wall, between the Minčeta fortress and Placa, and it certainly played a defensive role in time of need. The Franciscans had, and still have, a whole complex of buildings in this area. There is the big church on Placa, damaged slightly in 1667; the lower cloister, a magnificent late Romanesque work sculptured by Miho Brajkov from Bar (on the Montenegrian coast, south of Dubrovnik) in the first half of the fourteenth century; and, finally, the upper cloister, an elegant Gothic structure of great charm. In the lower cloister a pharmacy was opened in 1317, and, still in operation, it is one of the oldest in Europe (see Chapter IV).

The Dominican monastery and church, built during the fourteenth and fifteenth centuries on the eastern side of the city, were originally left outside the city walls. Like the Franciscan in the west, the Dominican monastery in the east had an even more pronounced defensive character. It was only in the middle of the fifteenth century that it was finally brought within the city by an extension of the eastern walls.

The monastery was built in the fifteenth-century Gothic style by local artists and remains almost unchanged. Like the Franciscan monastery, it contains important libraries and manuscript collections (see Chapter V). The Dominican church, however, survived only in part in its original form; much was added and changed later, but fortunately a number of precious paintings of Ragusan and other painters were preserved.

The small Church of Saint Savior, probably the most beautiful existing church in Dubrovnik, deserves special mention. Located near the Franciscan church on Placa, it was built in the Renaissance style by the Andrijić brothers, who erected it as a votive church after a strong earthquake in 1520. Earlier, in 1444, a bell tower approximately one hundred feet high was built at the eastern end of Placa, where it still stands.

In conclusion, the following facts must be emphasized. During the fourteenth and fifteenth centuries, Dubrovnik's walls and fortifications took shape, after the enlargement of the early walls in the second half of the thirteenth century. Inside these new walls a city was built in which streets and squares were organized according to a pre-established urban plan which called for straight lines wherever possible. A predominantly wooden city was changed by the beginning of the fifteenth century into a completely stone one, and inside this city luxurious private houses, one beautiful public palace, and a number of big and richly decorated churches and monasteries embellished the ambience with a mixture of Romanesque, Gothic, and Renaissance styles. Finally, all of this must be put in the context of the natural setting. With intense blue skies overhead and a deep, open sea surrounding part of the monumental walls, Dubrovnik—perched high on the rocks—offered then, as it does now, a unique view to the spectator from any side. Elegantly built and strongly fortified, the city was ready and able to move ahead toward new achievements in the succeeding centuries.

IV

Hygienic and Sanitation Measures

DUBROVNIK was one of the first cities in Europe to discover the importance of applying sanitary measures as a safeguard against infection and disease. The great attention paid to this aspect of life was reflected in a series of acts which, undertaken with courage and energy throughout the fourteenth and fifteenth centuries, improved in many ways the lives of Dubrovnik's inhabitants. Jorjo Tadić was right in writing that "Through the efforts of its citizens, Dubrovnik became pre-eminent in the field of hygiene."

To begin with, the statutes of Dubrovnik of 1272, indicate that lepers were living in a segregated area which, before the city was enlarged in the middle of the thirteenth century, was outside the walls. However, after the city was expanded to include that section, it was ordered that the "lepers must go and live at a distance from the city." They were sent to a place outside the walls, to the east, but they were not too strictly separated from the rest of the population. They were allowed to enter the city, and sometimes they gathered there in such large numbers that the government had to expel them by force. It seems that in time some lepers started organizing their quarters in many other parts of the state, while others continuously roamed around. The government and private persons tried to help them with money and other gifts. During the fifteenth century, however, the number of lepers fell sharply, and by 1472 only seventeen remained. In the sixteenth century there is no more mention of them in the archival documents, which suggests that they ceased to be a problem for Dubrovnik.

Leprosy was far from being the most dangerous disease in Dubrovnik. There were others much more ominous, and because of them the city had to take measures to protect itself. The main element in these efforts, of course, was the human one, that is to say, physicians and pharmacists. The first physician to be mentioned in the preserved documents of Dubrovnik was a *"magister Josephus,"* on August 14, 1280, and from that time until the end of the fifteenth century there is reference to about 110 physicians in the city. These men were divided into two large groups: physicians for internal diseases, who were called *magister medicus physicus* or later *doctor artis medicinae*; and those for external diseases, who were called *magister medicus plagarum* and later *magister medicus chirurgus*. A few of them had the title *medicinae professor* and were better paid in Dubrovnik, although the title indicated a practicing physician in a city having a medical college in which he taught, rather than a scholar. It is interesting to note that in the year 1325 a woman *medica* is mentioned, probably a midwife, while at the beginning of the fifteenth century *"magister Samuel Ebreus, medicus chirurgus"* was a practicing surgeon specializing in diseases of the eye.

The majority of physicians were Italians, more than sixty out of the total. The second most numerous group were Jews, numbering fourteen, followed by Spaniards, Greeks, Germans, and French. There were Slavic folk doctors too, some of them coming from the Balkan hinterland and using their skills mainly to heal hernias. The striking thing is that apparently there were no native Ragusan physicians in the city in the fourteenth and fifteenth centuries, in spite of the fact that a considerable number of young Ragusans studied in Italy, particularly Padua (see Chapter V). This was not due to unsatisfactory salaries, for the physicians in Dubrovnik were generally very well paid. The average annual salary in the fourteenth century was two hundred ducats for the *chirurgi* and up to four hundred ducats for the *physici*. In the fifteenth century these salaries were somewhat higher. There were, of course, physicians who were still better remunerated for their services, and some of them received free housing or extra money. If the physicians had a pharmacy, they were given an additional amount of money.

The earliest documents tell us that at first the physicians were allowed a fee of two Ragusan hyperperi from each patient, but from the beginning of the fourteenth century, when their salaries were increased, they were forbidden to accept fees from private persons, except foreigners. As for Ragusans, the physicians were obliged to treat them all—the count or rector, the archbishop and noblemen, priests, nuns, and friars, merchants, sailors, and peasants, men and women —without any compensation at all. Some physicians had to provide free medicine for their patients as well. Foreigners made individual contracts with physicians for the cure of their diseases. The contracts usually stipulated that the physician would not get his fee unless the patient was cured, and even the medicines he gave to the patient were not to be paid for if they did not produce the desired effect.

Many physicians developed extensive commercial practices in Dubrovnik and with various other regions. A number of them were sent by the Ragusan government to cure rulers and feudal lords in Bosnia and Serbia and later Ottoman governors of those lands. These physicians traveled with Ragusan ambassadors and merchants and frequently reached deep into the Balkan hinterland, where they stayed quite a while. One of the most interesting cases of this kind was that of "*Antonius medicus de Monteflore.*" He entered Ragusan service probably in 1329 and later was sent to Serbia. His testament, from 1337, provides a good picture of how a man of his profession spread widely his activities. Anthony bequeathed money for the building of a church in Prizren and to some priests in the same Serbian city. He also left money to a church in Ulcinj, a city on the Serbian coast, south of Dubrovnik, and to a church in Dubrovnik itself. Furthermore, he willed a large sum of money for the building of a hospital in his native Montefiore, near Ancona, in Italy, where he had other property. Among the things he owned in Serbia, he mentioned two suitcases, one horse, a carpet, and other things, but it is particularly notable that he had a coffer full of books which were supposed to be sent to Dubrovnik and then to his sister, probably in Montefiore.

At the time he went to Serbia, Anthony had taken with him fifteen ducats' worth of medicines for Nicolas Buća, an outstanding nobleman in the court of the Serbian king,

Stephen Dušan. Buća had five hundred ducats from the king to be paid to Anthony as salary for his work. The physician spent at least two and a half years in Serbia and took part in some very interesting political events, including a meeting between the Serbian king and the Byzantine emperor, Andronicus III Palaeologus.

On the other hand, there were a few instances of physicians coming to Dubrovnik from the East. For example, in 1458, Master Andrew from Constantinople was engaged for service in Dubrovnik. Before that, he had served awhile as physician to the Serbian despot, George Branković, and later he probably went to Italy. Two other Greek physicians worked in Dubrovnik between 1461 and 1480.

The fact that physicians moved between Dubrovnik and Italy on the one side and Dubrovnik and the Balkans on the other meant, of course, that still another link was forged between the East and the West. Again, as in trade, Dubrovnik served as a focal point. It must not be forgotten that physicians were far better educated than merchants. The best proof of their education is the books they owned. It is not possible to say what books were in the coffer of Anthony, but a document from 1418 gives us a list of thirty books which belonged to "the eminent doctor of medicine, Master Peter the physician, son of Master Albertinus from Camurata" (himself a prominent medical man in Dubrovnik). The list contains many medical works by Avicena, Hypocrates, Galienus, and others, and also Aristotle's *Testus Ethicorum* and *Liber Politicorum*, as well as "many and various grammatical books." There were other cases, all of them demonstrating the importance of physicians in the spreading of cultural influences wherever they went at the time.

Another group of people who must be mentioned in this connection are the barbers. Their role was very important, especially in the parts of the Republic of Dubrovnik removed from the city, and it remained so until the nineteenth century. Although they had no medical education, they performed a number of minor operations such as bloodletting, and their ability to cure patients with wounds was recognized. The government itself regarded the barbers as persons authorized to take care of the health of the people. Thus in 1312 the government gave a barber forty hyperperi above his annual salary for the medicines he gave out to his patients. He was not, however, allowed to take any money from them, either for curing them or for giving them medicines. Barbers took young men as apprentices to teach them "the barbers' and chirurgs' art," something that physicians never did.

After the physicians, the second most important group engaged in protecting the health of the Ragusans were the pharmacists. There is no doubt that people in ancient Dubrovnik and its neighborhood knew how to prepare medicines using medicinal herbs long before there was mention of the first pharmacists and pharmacies. This is a region where medicinal herbs abound. Besides, there were a number of Benedictine monasteries around Dubrovnik in which skills of this kind were well known. In the statutes of 1272 there is mention of medicinal herbs and trade in them. They were called *species*, and consequently the pharmacists later came to be known as *speciarii*. However, they sold not only medicinal herbs and medicines but many other articles as well. The first pharmacist was a Venetian, mentioned in 1301, and until the 1480's the pharmacists were almost exclusively Italians. Only toward the end of the fifteenth century did the first local pharmacists appear.

The government of Dubrovnik took constant care of the pharmacies and those in charge. The pharmacists were frequently given housing and shops by the state, but their salaries—when there were any—were much smaller than those of physicians. However, they engaged in commerce, both with Italy and with the Balkans, and from time to time went personally into those areas. Some of them became quite wealthy. For example, Martinus Johannis Richo inherited his pharmacy in Dubrovnik from his father, the Florentine Johannes Antonii Richo, who had come to Dubrovnik about 1405. When the son died in 1454, he left 5,216 ducats in cash and other articles, 416 ducats in pawned objects, mainly gold and silver, and more than 1,750 ducats in credits. Although the pharmacists did not occupy as important a place or play as prominent a role as did the physicians, they did contribute notably to the transmission of medical knowledge from Italy to Dubrovnik and, through Dubrovnik, at least partially to the Balkans. Indeed, the pharmacists took servants to whom they frequently taught their art. These were young men, mainly from Dubrovnik, though also from the hinterland, and from among them the first native pharmacists were most probably recruited.

The first two pharmacies organized in Dubrovnik are still operating. One of them is the pharmacy of the Franciscan monastery, founded in 1317 and therefore one of the oldest pharmacies functioning in Europe today. During its long life the pharmacy grew and moved several times, but always inside the monastery, where it is now. The second oldest pharmacy was started, according to reliable tradition, in 1420, as part of the "Major Hospital," but it is possible that it is considerably older, perhaps dating from the middle of the fourteenth century. Thus it is also one of the oldest still active pharmacies in Europe. As mentioned previously, the pharmacies were places where not only medicines but many other articles were sold to the public, and they therefore served as important centers of Ragusan trade as a whole.

What were the diseases which physicians, barbers, and pharmacists had to fight? Like all medieval cities, Dubrovnik was exposed to many sorts of epidemics, and the Ragusan chroniclers and analysts mention them as far back as the ninth century. Of course, it is impossible to verify their statements, but there can be no doubt that epidemics swept the city frequently. The greatest tragedy occurred when the bubonic plague of 1348 struck the city, the same plague which wrought havoc and caused thousands of deaths throughout Europe. In Dubrovnik this "unheard-of and incurable disease," as one document puts it, began in December, 1347, and lasted for seven months. The documents suggest that an average of twenty or more people died every day and that the total dead included 110 priests. On the whole, according to the best local chronicler, Restić, 6,000 common people died, in addition to 273 patricians. It seems probable that the numbers in both cases are somewhat exaggerated, but the population loss to Dubrovnik certainly was terrible. As a result, the Major Council lowered the age at which male patricians could enter as full-fledged members from twenty to eighteen,

and a series of measures were taken to stimulate the preservation of the population. Craftsmen were allowed to settle
in the city and were exempt from taxes for five years; those
coming within one year of the decrees were even promised
monetary rewards; all who had been punished for debts and
other financial offenses were allowed to return safely to
Dubrovnik.

Dubrovnik recovered, but this was not the only epidemic to
hit the city. About ten years later, new outbursts of the plague
took place, and a second big sweep came in 1363. It was not
as severe as the one in 1348—it lasted only about three months
and took the lives of about three hundred persons—but the
government increased its efforts to attract new inhabitants
into the city. In the next decades smaller or bigger outbursts
of the plague were a frequent occurrence, particularly in
1374 and 1400. The situation continued unchanged into the
fifteenth century, with big outbursts occurring almost regularly in each decade. Many of these and other waves of the
plague swept not only through Dubrovnik but also through
the whole territory of the republic. In several instances, the
plague first entered the peripheral regions of the state, and
thus in a few cases the Ragusans were able to limit it to the
islands.

The bubonic plague, however, was not the only disease
which affected life in Dubrovnik. There were many others.
Leprosy has been mentioned already; still another problem
was malaria. The city itself was not threatened by it, but the
region of Rijeka Dubrovačka, behind the mountain, where
there was a river, felt the effects of this disease. The situation
was particularly difficult in Ston, the second most important

locality in the republic and the seat of government for the Pelješac peninsula. Ston was surrounded by shallow sea and water channels, and it was an important center for the production of salt. It remained one of the worst malaria areas on the whole Adriatic coast for centuries. The Ragusan patricians, in spite of their dedication to duty, hated having to go to Ston to work, and sending a patrician there for a few months' forced stay became a punitive measure used against unruly members of the elite.

Venereal diseases seem to have arrived in Dubrovnik only at the beginning of the sixteenth century, after the French armies spread them in Italy. However, before then there were physicians in Dubrovnik who declared that they knew how to cure infirmities of the genitals, but it is not possible to know what was really meant. Of course, the reason for venereal disease was prostitution, which always existed in Dubrovnik, as elsewhere (see Chapter VI). It must be noted here that in many cases, when there is mention of an epidemic or disease in documents or chronicles, there is not sufficient information to identify it exactly.

Apart from hiring physicians, barbers, and pharmacists, the inhabitants of Dubrovnik looked for additional ways to cope with the maladies with which they were afflicted. An important step was taken with the institution of the quarantine in 1377. This was done, no doubt, under the impact of the plagues, particularly the one in 1374, and also following the example of the Venetians, who had initiated a similar measure in that year. The first quarantine area was instituted in Cavtat and on the small island of Mrkan nearby. It was meant for Ragusans as well as for foreigners coming from contaminated regions. Isolation was to be complete and was to last one month. In 1397 the island of Mljet was included within the quarantine territory. A special committee was set up to control the movement of persons coming from suspected infectious regions, and severe punishments, including fines, jailing, flogging, branding, and cutting off an ear were introduced. Twenty years later, in 1416, and again in 1422 measures were taken to ensure the proper operation of the government during epidemics, while in 1426 special functionaries, the *officiales cazamortuorum*, were put in charge of sanitation. From that time, they were responsible for administering procedures to protect the health of persons within the republic, and they exerted considerable influence.

The quarantine system and other measures were constantly improved in the fifteenth century. New places for confinement were found, particularly on some small islands and in an area not far from the city itself, at Dance, where a wall which still exists was built in 1466 to isolate the sick from the rest of the population. It must be noted here, however, that at this time Dubrovnik had to handle a different kind of problem.

Constant warfare in Herzegovina in the immediate vicinity of Dubrovnik, between the Herzegovinian and Ottoman armies, as well as internal conflicts, had left the region devastated and poor, and large numbers of people moved toward Dubrovnik several times in the 1450's and 1460's to escape famine. Thus, toward the end of 1453 and the beginning of 1454—at a time when Dubrovnik was at war with the Herzeg Stephen Vukčić-Kosača—the number of hungry persons from Herzegovina who had arrived in Dubrovnik and were roaming around the city was so big that the government decided to expel all who did not have a dwelling in Dubrovnik, but this was difficult to achieve. To prevent additional infiltration of such persons into the city, armed guards were put at the gates to repel them. In the autumn of 1454 hundreds of starving Herzegovinians were trying to find food and shelter on the coast in and around the Republic of Dubrovnik. Many of them were begging for transportation to Italy, while others were dying from hunger, according to Ragusan descriptions. But Dubrovnik itself, through guards and other measures, prevented them from entering its walls, thus preserving its health and hygienic standards.

Later, in the sixteenth century, a lazaret was built on the island of Lokrum, and the large lazaret which still stands in the eastern suburb of Ploče was built only in the seventeenth century. These measures certainly helped to lessen, if not to avert completely, the effect of epidemics in Dubrovnik. It must be added that the Ragusans took steps to protect their territories from the sea side too. The first such actions were mentioned in the second half of the fourteenth century, and they continued later. Ships were sent for quarantine to the island of Mljet, to Lokrum, or, if their cargoes were particularly precious, near the harbor of Dubrovnik itself. Sometimes they were simply forbidden to enter any Ragusan port and were sent away. Captains and sailors who lied when examined by the *cazamorti* about their origin or who violated the quarantine were punished by fine, imprisonment, and the cutting off of their ears.

Besides the procedures set up to provide protection from diseases brought from the outside, Dubrovnik had to take measures inside the city to increase the welfare of its inhabitants. As described earlier (see Chapter III), the plan of the city favored the circulation of air because of the straight streets meeting at right angles. The removal of wooden houses, particularly at the beginning of the fifteenth century, not only increased the resistance of the city to fires but also improved its hygienic standards. But Dubrovnik, like all medieval cities, suffered from dirty streets which served as gutters and as repositories of garbage, as well as places in which animals could circulate together with men. The fact that the vast majority of streets in Dubrovnik were narrow only increased the problems. Although the Ragusan government very early enacted legislation to regulate public hygiene and punished violators of its orders, it was only in 1388 that a man was appointed with the specific duty of supervising the cleanliness of the city. Probably before that date, the main street, Placa, and some squares were paved with brick. However, in 1389 a special committee of patricians was set up to oversee the paving of Dubrovnik's streets, and special measures were taken to ensure sufficient bricks for this work.

The year 1407 was of special importance to the improvement of public hygiene on Dubrovnik's streets. The government decided to undertake two related tasks: the paving of all streets and the regulation of the draining of water from them. Until this time, clean and dirty waters flowed through the streets toward Placa, the lowest part of the city, and created pools there which obviously were not only unpleasant but also a threat to the health of the inhabitants. Besides, whenever there was a heavy rain, the lower part of Dubrovnik was inundated and transformed into a swamp. The 1407 regulations were guided by two basic principles: to prevent all the water from flowing toward Placa while at the same time draining it from that part of the city, and to guide all the water toward the sea, partly through the eastern and partly through the western side of the city. The plan of the streets and the sloping ground facilitated the execution of this scheme, which combined the utilization of natural advantages with adroit human intervention.

It was certainly in connection with their efforts to improve sanitation and to facilitate the functioning of the new drainage system that the Ragusans decided, also in 1407, to pave all the streets in the city. All the streets were listed, and every year a certain number of them was selected by lot for paving. The expenses were shared, half paid by the state and half by the owners of houses or land on these streets. Some streets were paved exclusively in stone, while in others inhabitants declared their preference for stone or brick. If the inhabitants of streets that were not yet chosen wanted to have theirs paved ahead of schedule, they could do so with the same sharing of expenses. The main work of paving the streets and squares was completed in about thirty years, but constant care and improvement through centuries were required, particularly as long as parts of the city were paved with brick.

After making improvements in the streets and with a continuing awareness of hygienic standards, the Ragusans felt the need to organize a garbage-collecting service. The first four street sweepers were engaged by the government in 1415. Their duty was not only to collect the garbage and take it out of the city but also to observe and report anybody who threw garbage in the streets. Shopkeepers and house owners were ordered to sweep and clean in front of their shops and houses every Saturday after work. All of this, of course, does not mean that Dubrovnik became a model of cleanliness. On the contrary, repeated governmental legislation, threats, and decisions throughout the fifteenth century prove that the Ragusans still did not work hard enough to maintain proper hygienic conditions in their city. However, there is no doubt that the concentrated efforts of the government at the beginning of the century made Dubrovnik one of the better places to live in contemporary Europe, and particularly in the Mediterranean world.

The next important steps in the improvement of living conditions in Dubrovnik were taken in the year 1436. One was the setting up of a sewage system and the other the decision to build an aqueduct. In 1436 detailed plans were drawn up for a sewage system which would carry all waste into the sea. The completed system solved many problems which the city had faced for a long time. It works to this day and, by general agreement, was the most functional system that could have been constructed under the circumstances prevailing in Dubrovnik.

The second big advance was the building of the aqueduct. Dubrovnik, by its position, was always faced with the problem of an adequate water supply. There was no water anywhere around the old city on the rock or the new, enlarged one. The Ragusans at first drained water from the roofs into cisterns in or near their houses. The state also dug a number of public wells, probably after the city expanded and was surrounded by new walls. Some wells were in the street which to this day is called Od puča, "the street of the wells"; they contained filtered sea water which until relatively recent times was used by the people. However, with the growth in population, the need for new quantities of water was soon felt. Government efforts to dig additional and bigger wells were not adequate, particularly with the increase in textile production, which required ever larger amounts of water for the industry and for the imported craftsmen and workers it employed. The government tried to remedy the situation by organizing the shipping of water from sources a few miles east from the city. The water was carried on boats which, by governmental decree, had to pick up the water and bring it into the city in a pre-established manner.

Nevertheless, the crisis became increasingly acute, and finally, in June, 1436, the government accepted an offer by the Italian architect, Onofrio de la Cava, and his partner to build an aqueduct. They were to bring the water to Dubrovnik from a source about ten miles away, on the northern side of Srdj Mountain. In great detail they spelled out how the conduits were to be built. The two masters were supposed to hire one or two local craftsmen who could learn how to build other aqueducts and how to maintain this one. The government offered to provide certain materials to the Italians, and Onofrio and his partner were under contract to complete the whole construction and bring the water into the city by October, 1437, that is, within one year and four months, for the price of 8,250 ducats.

The work seems to have lasted a little longer, until 1438, and to have been somewhat more expensive than planned, but the results were excellent. The aqueduct was so masterfully made that it not only supplied Dubrovnik with all the necessary water in the fifteenth century but continues to function to the present time (a new aqueduct was built only a few years ago to supplement the old one). Although he had a partner in this work, it is Onofrio who is remembered as the builder of the aqueduct. This, no doubt, is because he spent a long time in Dubrovnik and participated very actively in other works (see Chapter III) and especially because he erected two magnificent fountains in the city after the aqueduct was finished. Between 1438 and 1440, Onofrio built the big fountain near the western entrance to the city, and a little later he built a small fountain near the Church of Saint Blaise. Both were commissioned by the government and both exist and function today. Thus Onofrio's works provided Dubrovnik with fresh water and with two beautiful fountains which are ornaments to the city.

Another important element in improving and maintaining satisfactory health conditions in Dubrovnik was the provision for an adequate food supply. Dubrovnik was built on extremely poor, barren land from which very little food could be obtained. In early epochs, the inhabitants cultivated some land near the city and paid a tribute to the nearby Slavs for permission to do so. They also had vineyards on small islands nearby, but all of this proved to be insufficient as soon as the population increased. Fishing certainly was an additional means of obtaining food, but a limited one. Therefore, it is not surprising that the Ragusans engaged very early in importing food. Documents from the end of the thirteenth century—that is, from the time documents were systematically preserved—show that this activity was well organized and tightly controlled by the government.

This was particularly true of the importation of cereals. For this vital food, Dubrovnik depended completely on imports. A special committee of three patricians was in charge of providing the city with necessary grains—foremost among them barley, millet, and wheat—and the government directly decided on all important matters connected with this trade. Information on crops and the availability of cereals was eagerly collected, and the government always did its best to maintain good relations with states and regions from which cereals were imported. The most important areas were southern Italy and Sicily, but grains were imported also from Albania, the region of Ancona, western Asia Minor, the Black Sea basin, and later from parts of Greece and other places. All of this means that, once the Ottomans became masters of Asia Minor and southeast Europe, Dubrovnik depended very heavily on their good will for its cereal provisions. This was an additional, but very substantial, reason for its efforts to find and keep a *modus vivendi* with the conquerors.

The Ragusans organized the importing of cereals in such a way that shipowners knew a year ahead of time when their turn would come to carry grains to the city. They were strictly controlled and severely punished if they disobeyed orders. In emergencies the government would simply order all Ragusan ships to transport cereals, would give prizes to importers, and would free foreign importers from customs fees. Foreigners took a relatively small part in this trade, but in times of great need the government did not hesitate to confiscate cereals from foreign ships in the Ragusan port. The trade in cereals inside Dubrovnik was either free and handled by private merchants or controlled and organized by the state. This depended on the available quantities in Dubrovnik and the needs of the city. When necessary, the government took full control and even established rationing. For the preservation of cereals, the Ragusans used their warehouse (*fundichus*). When this proved insufficient, at the beginning of the fifteenth century, they started digging special pits and storing grains in them. The capacity of these pits was about 1,200 tons. Gradually they were enlarged, covered, and improved, all of which eventually led to the building of the big edifice which to this day is called Rupe—"the pits." Owing to the excellent organization of cereal provisioning, Dubrovnik very rarely suffered from famine as many other cities and regions did. Even in the local chronicles and annals, which tend to exaggerate dramatic events, there are only eight mentions of famines in more than five hundred years, and it has been proved that at least three of these caused no real difficulty for Dubrovnik.

Cereals, of course, were not the only foodstuffs eaten by the Ragusans. The government saw to it that the city always had sufficient quantities of vegetables. Small quantities could be obtained in Ragusan territory, and the remainder was imported. Fresh vegetables were grown near the city—notably cabbage and broccoli, specialties of Dubrovnik to this day. Meat was imported mainly from the hinterland, rich in small cattle, and it was consumed fresh, smoked, or salted. Fish was another important nutriment, frequently preserved with salt. Fish was also highly appreciated by the rulers and lords of Bosnia and Serbia and later by Ottomans who became Ragusan neighbors. The government of Dubrovnik, whenever possible, tried to please all of them by providing them with fish. Cheese was another food very much used in Dubrovnik, whether it was made in Ragusan territory or imported from the Balkans.

The cuisine of Dubrovnik required the accompaniment of olive oil, which many olive trees on Ragusan estates provided. However, the quantities were usually insufficient, and olive oil had to be imported from Apulia. The government of Dubrovnik paid much attention to oil and even more to wine. In fact, after cereals, wine—considered good for the health— seems to have been the most important article of Ragusan nutrition. It was found in every house, hospital, monastery, and even jail. The consumption apparently was considerable, and when domestic production was insufficient, the government organized and strictly controlled the traffic and importing of wine from Italy. Even the transportation of wine from the Ragusan islands and Pelješac or Konavli into the city was constantly surveyed and taxed. Besides the ordinary grapes, there was a special one from which the famous Maluasia wine was made. This wine—presumably from Greek vines brought from Monembasia—was specially prized, and the Ragusans sometimes sent it as a present to a cardinal in Rome, a prince in an Italian city, or a doge in Venice. However, with time its quantity and quality declined, and it lost its role in Ragusan diplomacy.

Two humanitarian institutions which played an important role in Dubrovnik should be mentioned in conclusion. The first was the hospital for the poor. The decision to build such an institution was made in 1347, and consequently the one which exists to this day in a slightly changed form (as a home for elderly people) is one of the oldest in Western Europe. It was called *Hospitale magnum*—"the big hospital"—and many Ragusans left money to it in their wills. But the sick could not enter here, for there were separate charitable institutions for them. In 1540 the *Hospitale magnum* was transformed into a general hospital, called *Domus Christi*, and this was the beginning of the Ragusan hospital existing now. At first, only men were accepted into the new hospital, while sick women continued to live in charity homes, very numerous in the city throughout the fourteenth and the following centuries. These institutions, like many other charitable activities, were supported through private efforts and donations, which were always abundant in Dubrovnik.

The second important humanitarian institution was the orphanage. Founded in 1432, this *Hospitale misericordiae* was one of the earliest in Western Europe. There were, indeed, many illegitimate and poor children in Dubrovnik. It must be emphasized that Ragusans did not hide the fact that they had illegitimate children. On the contrary, they cared for them very well. Many of them helped such children get an education and jobs, and almost regularly in testaments these children were mentioned and their fathers left them money or other gifts. This recognition of illegitimate children went so far that, at the beginning of the fifteenth century, illegitimate children of patricians started taking their fathers' names and wearing external signs of nobility—a thing which could not possibly be accepted—and in 1413 it was officially proposed to the Major Council to prohibit such practices (see Chapter VI).

This does not mean, however, that all such children were

happy and well cared for in Dubrovnik. As elsewhere, there were many cases of neglected and even murdered illegitimate children, as well as many poor children. This is why the orphanage was created and detailed plans for its functioning and financing were made. The government closely supervised this institution and tried to improve its living conditions. The orphanage, sometime during its existence, supposedly received pregnant women and enabled them to give birth to their children, whom they would then leave at the orphanage. At the same time it accepted already born children. In both instances complete secrecy of identity was guaranteed. Ragusans could adopt children from the orphanage beginning in the fifteenth century, and peasants particularly took advantage of the opportunity to do so.

With these institutions demonstrating humanitarian sensibility and serving practical purposes as well; with one of the first pharmacies in Europe and pharmacists and physicians to take care of the health of its inhabitants; with quarantine and other measures constantly enforced against diseases and epidemics; with the paving of streets and squares and the building of sewage and drainage systems and of the aqueduct to improve hygiene; and with constant care for essential food supplies, Dubrovnik undoubtedly achieved one of the highest standards of health and sanitation protection in contemporary Europe. Moreover, in this field, as in others, Dubrovnik played an important role in the transmission of achievements between the East and the West. Indeed, much of what it did was done under the influence of Italian models, while at the same time Dubrovnik served as a model and as a reliable source of medical help for the Balkan hinterland.

V

Intellectual Life and Culture

EVALUATING the intellectual life and cultural development of a medieval city is probably the most difficult part of the complex task of describing the life of the city as a whole. The elements which compose the picture of the intellectual activity in a city are numerous and are not always easy to identify. The influences are diverse, unequal in their intensity, and frequently contradictory in their effect. All of this holds true of a city on the crossroads between the East and the West at a time when both areas were undergoing dynamic and profound changes and when the city itself was very rapidly developing. Another problem, of course, is the available source material from which the intellectual and cultural life of Dubrovnik can be seen and evaluated. Very little can be said for the period before the 1270's since there are almost no extant documents for that epoch and what few have survived do not deal with the aspect of life which interests us here.

It can be safely asserted that a new spirit in Dubrovnik, a new awareness of the civic life inside its walls, developed in the second half of the thirteenth century. Two important manifestations of this new spirit confirm this view: the writing of the statutes of the city and the beginning of the preservation of state documents. The statutes were written in 1272. They reflect the situation in the city and its administration as it had developed up to that time, but they also contain decisions that affected the future growth of the Commune of Dubrovnik, its foreign relations, and its commerce. The mere fact that the statutes were written indicates the existence of a new concept of the city and its life, a concept very much influenced, no doubt, by what was going on in the Italian cities across the Adriatic.

The second extremely important development, coming a little later than the statutes, was the beginning of the systematic preservation of the documents by the Commune; in fact, this was the start of what are today the famous Historical Archives of Dubrovnik. Jorjo Tadić correctly evaluated them by saying that in these archives "in a relatively small space, there are collected, one could say almost condensed, many more important historical materials—not only concerning Dubrovnik —than in many other large, even the largest archives. This is one of the features of the archives of Dubrovnik which make them one of the world's outstanding collections of sources, particularly in Southeastern Europe and on the Mediterranean."

The year 1278 marks the approximate beginning of this important collection, but there are separate acts from long before that year. The oldest document preserved in the archives is a papal bull of 1022, by which the Ragusan Bishopric was elevated to Archbishopric. The series in which this document is kept, *Acta Sanctae Mariae Maioris*, contains separate acts from the eleventh to the nineteenth centuries. Only one other document is from the eleventh century, but the acts from the two following centuries are much more numerous. From 1278 on, there are thousands of volumes in which documents covering all aspects of everyday life in the city and its international relations were recorded and preserved. The archives of Dubrovnik today contain about 7,000 volumes, divided into 92 series, as well as some 100,000 separate acts. All together they constitute an almost limitless wealth of data not only on Dubrovnik itself but on the Balkans, Italy, Albania, Greece, Spain, Hungary, and, to a smaller degree, practically all European countries in the period from 1278 until 1808.

Both the statutes and the beginning of the archives reflect the prosperity and improvement of life in Dubrovnik. While the statutes—and additions to them, as well as other later laws—have considerable importance for the study of Dubrovnik, there can be no doubt that the archival documents are the basic source of information on all aspects of the city's life and change. Those documents were written primarily in Latin, Italian, and Slavic (using the Cyrillic alphabet), with a small number in Greek, French, Spanish, and other languages. There are also several thousand Ottoman documents in Dubrovnik. It is not surprising, however, that most of these acts were written in Latin, since that was the official language of the state and remained such until the downfall of the republic. It should be noted, nevertheless, that a specific Romanic language, Old Ragusan, was still used in Dubrovnik. At this time it was used only by tradition in internal affairs of the city, but even in that domain its role was diminishing.

Italian was widespread, not only because of the presence of many Italians in Dubrovnik, but also because it was the commercial language of the Mediterranean, owing to the pre-eminence of Italian commercial city republics, particularly Venice, in the Mediterranean trade. Ragusan merchants knew Italian and wrote letters in that language. The government itself sometimes corresponded with its ambassadors in Italian.

The slavicization of Dubrovnik, however, had begun very early, probably in the tenth century, and was completed by the second half of the thirteenth century. As early as the first half of the 1200's there was a Slavic chancellery in Dubrovnik. Its chancellors, who read and wrote in the Slavic Cyrillic alphabet, handled the correspondence of Dubrovnik with the rulers and feudal lords of the Balkan hinterland, who knew no Latin or Italian. The first Cyrillic document in Dubrovnik was the treaty with Bosnia in 1189, and later Cyrillic documents became quite numerous, including not only official correspondence but also private acts and letters from individual merchants. This is only one indication of the increasing slavicization of Dubrovnik; there are many others. One of the oldest streets existing today under the name Prijeko, meaning "across," was already called Prijeki put, "the road across," in the 1280's. Outside but close to the city there is a hill, Ilijina glavica, whose modern name is found in documents of the same epoch in exactly the same form. Hundreds of personal names, including those of members of patrician families, testify to the successful process of slavicization in the thirteenth century.

There is interesting and direct proof that, although the

official language of Dubrovnik was Latin, the population spoke the Slavic language at the end of the thirteenth and the beginning of the fourteenth century. For example, in 1284 a man fleeing from the police escaped to a boat in the harbor, and the scribe, in the Latin description of this event, wrote that the people of Dubrovnik were screaming "*Podhi sbogo*," a purely Slavic farewell (*"Podji s Bogom*," or "Go with God"). In addition, in the early decades of the fourteenth century, the government repeatedly ordered its town criers to announce decrees and news to the population in Latin and in Slavic. Slavic words gradually penetrated in increasing numbers into Latin and Italian inventories of such things as household goods and clothing, where they were written with roman letters. In the fifteenth century these words appeared with growing frequency in judicial decisions, relating many obscenities and various offences hurled between persons in everyday quarrels. In the acts written in the chancellery of Ston especially, there are not only signatures and single words but entire phrases written in Slavic, usually in Cyrillic letters.

The slavicization of patricians, who for a while had emphasized their alleged Roman origins, gradually advanced to such a degree that by the fifteenth century they were using the Slavic language even in governmental councils. In fact, it became necessary for the government to forbid this practice in 1472.

It must be noted, however, that slavicization was not in any way the result of a planned effort in education but the consequence of a natural process of demographic growth, created by the constant influx of the nearby Slavic populations. Education could never have brought about the slavicization, for it was oriented in quite a different direction. Literacy in Dubrovnik was relatively widespread from early times, because it was a prerequisite for successful trade. With the development of commercial operations and an increase in their worth, the need for literacy and some knowledge of mathematics was felt even in lower social groups.

There were private teachers in Dubrovnik, particularly priests and individuals from Italy, but the first mention of a teacher appointed officially is from March 6, 1333. The government unanimously decided that, "since in the city of Dubrovnik there is no teacher to instruct boys in grammar, ten hyperperi be given for one year from the communal property to Master Nicolas from Verona, who must teach boys in grammar and other sciences he knows and to write, and that he be paid according to the habitude of the city." This is an indication that the ten hyperperi were given for habitation (as in later cases of other teachers) and that there was a previously established way of remunerating the teachers. Therefore, Nicolas probably was not the first. From this time on, there was regular mention of teachers being engaged by the government to instruct children in Dubrovnik. Their teaching consisted mainly of Latin grammar and, of course, writing and reading. The salaries of the teachers were rather low at the beginning. The first one, mentioned in 1346, consisted of only twenty hyperperi, but the teachers were authorized to accept payments from their pupils. However, financial remunerations rapidly increased. By 1348 the count was allowed to pay up to forty hyperperi per year to "Master Anthony, who was made doctor of grammar," and in 1362 the Ragusans were offering up to thirty ducats (sixty hyperperi) for a teacher. These men were also allowed to accept payments from their pupils, but on a smaller, controlled scale.

The teachers came mostly from Italy, but there were local men, particularly priests, who also served in this capacity. It is quite probable that some of them taught Cyrillic script, but the only such case confirmed by documentary evidence was that of "Nicolas the Bulgarian," in 1390–92, who was called "master of Slavic letters" and who taught "Slavic letters." The Italian teachers were recruited mainly in Venice, but they came from many parts of Italy. An interesting letter in 1381 from the Ragusan government to a patrician who was studying in Padua, asking him to find a teacher to send to Dubrovnik, describes very well what kind of man Dubrovnik wanted and what he was expected to do. He was to be "a good master of grammar, who will be a good grammarian, positive and true, of good habits and a good and honest way of life, and aged from thirty to forty years or thereabout." He was to be offered the enormous salary of one hundred ducats a year and could be engaged for two years at once. His duties would be "to teach well, solicitously, and assiduously all the pupils, citizens, and inhabitants of Dubrovnik in grammar as well as in reading and writing and to improve their habits, without accepting any payment from those pupils." The prospective teacher was to be told that fathers and relatives of the pupils would be grateful for his work and would honor him adequately.

There were parents, however, who were not fully satisfied with the education their sons could acquire in school, and they made separate agreements with private teachers for additional training. An example of such an agreement is the one made in 1413 between "Master Lucas from Šibenik, rector of the schools," and an Albanian priest whose nephew Lucas was supposed to teach "to read, explain, and translate [that is, in Italian] Donatus and Cato and to remember from Donatus what will be possible to the intellect" of the young man. In addition, the boy was to learn how to read and to remember various grammatical rules. All of this Lucas was supposed to achieve as quickly and as well as possible for the very small salary of only sixteen hyperperi. In time the need for a higher standard of teaching became so strong that in 1433 the government decided to establish a sort of high school, separate from the existing grammar school. It is therefore justified to say that the gymnasium existing in Dubrovnik today is the continuation of the high school established in 1433.

The old grammar school continued to offer classes taught by teachers, while for the high school the Ragusans began hiring professors from Italy who had varying amounts of humanistic education. Certainly the most important among them was Philippus de Diversis de Quartigianis, a man from Lucca who served from 1434 to 1440 as the principal of the Ragusan high school. He was a "master of grammar, rhetoric, logic, and philosophy" for "adult and non-adult pupils." In spite of these high titles, de Diversis seems to have been less than successful in Dubrovnik, and he complained that the Ragusans were more interested in practical than in theoretical knowledge. He left, however, a valuable description of Dubrovnik in his work *Situs aedificiorum, politiae et lauda-*

bilium consuetudinum inclytae civitatis Ragusii, or "The Site of the Buildings, Policies, and Praiseworthy Habits of the Illustrious City of Ragusium."

Another interesting teacher was Daniel Clarus from Parma, to whom the famous Aldus Manutius dedicated his *"editio princeps"* of Aristophanes' comedies in 1498. This happened during Clarus' stay in Dubrovnik, 1485–1505. At the same time, Elias Lampridius Crijević, a Ragusan who had achieved vast fame as a humanist and had been crowned in Rome as *"poeta laureatus,"* served as teacher in his native city from 1497 until 1504 and again from 1510 until 1520.

The Ragusans were evidently trying to get the best men they could to teach their children and were rather successful in their efforts. Although the impact of these teachers in Dubrovnik was certainly considerable, illiteracy and ignorance did not disappear from the city, nor did education in general attain a very high level. The best proof of the continuing illiteracy, even within the ranks of the patriciate, is found in the decision of the Major Council in 1455 that thereafter no patrician could occupy a position in or outside the city unless he was able to read and write, "for those who do not know how to read and write should rather be governed, than govern others, and it is of no honor to that administration or government that has in its ranks an ignorant man, unskilled in reading and writing." There can be no doubt, however, that throughout the fourteenth and fifteenth centuries there was a considerable effort within Dubrovnik to improve education, that this effort bore results, and that in this activity, too, Dubrovnik was on the watershed of two cultures, the Italian in the West and the Slavic in the East.

Apart from teachers, many other experts and specialists came to Dubrovnik from Italy. We have already spoken of physicians and pharmacists (see Chapter IV). A number of priests and friars came from Italy, and it is of particular importance that many Ragusan archbishops were Italians. Another group was the notaries and chancellors. Their role in Dubrovnik, as in any developed medieval city, was very valuable and went considerably beyond their immediate tasks in the notary or chancellery, extending into the diplomatic field especially. Being generally highly respected men, they were frequently involved in delicate diplomatic missions. More importantly, however, the notaries and chancellors brought humanistic ideas to Dubrovnik which they learned while living and being educated in Italy. Thus they contributed very much to the stirring of the new humanistic spirit in Dubrovnik. This can be observed in the Latin of documents and letters that they wrote. It became much more elaborate as the notaries tried to imitate the writings of classical Latin authors. In addition, an increasing number of quotations from ancient writers were included in various acts, particularly in testaments. While testaments from the fourteenth century were usually simple and straightforward, those from the fifteenth century—especially the testaments of patricians and priests—abounded in quotations in Latin, within Italian texts, from the Bible and from classical sources. The handwriting of the chancellors changed and became clearly more individualistic and freer from established rules.

Another proof of the penetration of the humanistic spirit in Dubrovnik is the latinization of personal names, mainly among patricians. Thus in the fifteenth century there were

Ragusan noblemen named Pompeius, Scipio, and so forth. Also, there were cases in which family names of patricians were translated from Italian into Latin form. It must be said, however, that this transmission of Italian humanistic influences into Dubrovnik was not only the result of Italians coming to that city. There were many young Ragusans, mostly patricians, who went to Italy, mainly to Padua, to get an education at the university there. We have already mentioned a case of this kind in 1381, but such stays in Italy were much more frequent in the fifteenth century. For example, in 1464 a nobleman left orders in his testament for all his books to be given to his grandson who "has started working on the study of letters and for this reason is staying at Padua"; in the following year another patrician left 259 hyperperi "to the college of Padua or Bologna" if it were established that he and his brother had illegally taken something from these colleges. In September, 1465, the canon and nobleman Dominicus Gučetić who was preparing to go to study in Italy, wrote his testament in which he gave an interesting explanation for his decision to undertake this activity at a not-so-young age: "I wish to appear at the tribunal of the Supreme Judge not in any other way but with a purified and clean conscience, but I have soiled it from the earliest memories, and not having ability nor possibility of unsoiling it otherways, I intend to do it through study and through other, very adequate means." Many other Ragusans studied elsewhere in Italy and even in Paris, and their contribution to Dubrovnik's culture was certainly quite substantial.

Some of these people became prominent not only in Dubrovnik but in the Western world as well. Three among them deserve special mention: Ivan Stojković, Ivan Gazul, and Benko Kotruljević. All were born about 1400. Ivan Stojković (Johannes de Staiis), son of a poor shoemaker, became a Dominican friar and was sent on a government scholarship to Paris to study at the Sorbonne. His performance was excellent, and he managed to ascend rapidly in the ecclesiastical ranks. Having become first an important figure at the papal court at Rome, he later played one of the leading roles in the Basle Council and also greatly helped the Ragusans in obtaining the concession for navigation to Egypt and Syria (see Chapter II).

As envoy of the Basle Council, Stojković traveled to Constantinople to seek the union of the Eastern and the Western churches. He was certainly picked for this job because of his knowledge of the Slavic language and of the Balkan situation. Stojković profited by his two-year stay in Constantinople by having theological and classical Greek works copied for him which he carried back to Basle. In Constantinople, Stojković had discussions with Patriarch Joseph II, a Bulgarian by origin, with whom he spoke Slavic. The Ragusan government profited by Stojković's stay in the Byzantine capital and asked him to intervene with Emperor John VIII to obtain commercial privileges for Dubrovnik. Stojković did, but nothing came of this attempt because of other circumstances. However, this is another proof that Stojković's links with his homeland remained very strong even after he was elevated to high positions in the church and had established a reputation as a prominent humanist and bibliophile, as well as an ecclesiastical diplomat and dignitary. Stojković stressed his Slavic origins also during his long disputations with the

Bohemian Hussite representatives in Basle. But this outstanding man died young, shortly after becoming a cardinal, in 1444, apparently leaving a large number of theological treatises and perhaps a description of his trip to Constantinople.

Ivan Gazul (Johannes Gazulus) was born about 1400, probably in Albania and certainly of Albanian Catholic parents. He spent most of his life in Dubrovnik, considered himself to be a Ragusan, and was seen as such by others. Gazul became a priest very young and was educated in Dubrovnik and Padua, where he obtained a doctorate in philosophy. He started very early performing important diplomatic missions for the Ragusan government, visiting the pope in Rome, the German emperor, the Hungarian king, prominent Hungarian feudal lords, and others. During his travels in Italy, he established many contacts with humanists and scholars, particularly those working in the field of astronomy. Everywhere he went, Gazul bought books and brought them back to Dubrovnik, thus building a valuable private library that would play an important role in Dubrovnik's cultural life. A prominent bibliophile and astronomer, Gazul acquired such fame that in 1459 he was invited by the Hungarian and Croatian king, Mattias Corvinus, to come to his court "with the books of his profession," an honor that Gazul refused because of his age and poor health. He died in 1465, and his prestige in Dubrovnik is best shown by the way he was called in his testament: "The venerable Master Johannes Gazulus, doctor of arts and most illustrious astronomer."

The third important figure in this group was Benko Kotruljević (Bencius de Cotruglio), a Ragusan who began studying in Italy, never finished his studies, but managed nevertheless to acquire a sound knowledge of classical history and philosophy. As a merchant, he obtained vast practical experience and traveled throughout the western Mediterranean. In 1451 he settled in Naples and became an important figure in the court of the Neapolitan Aragonese king, Alphons V. Kotruljević wrote a botanical work, now lost, and in 1458 a book in Italian: *On Commerce and the Perfect Merchant.* This was the first attempt ever made to deal in a scholarly way with the problem of the origins of commerce, its nature, and its many aspects and techniques (credit, exchange, deposits, bookkeeping by double entry, and so forth). The work is valuable also because it emphasizes the views of the emerging modern citizenry on nature, education, religion, and social problems. In addition, Kotruljević sharply criticized his conservative contemporaries and fellow citizens. Although he spent most of his life in Italy, other members of his family stayed in Dubrovnik, and his links with them and the city were never severed. In 1458 he became Dubrovnik's consul in Naples. In the same year King Alphons V died and was succeeded by King Ferdinand, during whose rule Kotruljević apparently climbed even higher in the royal favor, becoming chief of the royal mint. He died in 1469.

Books, of course, are one of the most important indicators of the cultural level achieved by any human community. This holds true for Dubrovnik, as it does for all other medieval cities. As early as the first half of the fourteenth century, Ragusan testaments mentioned books, mainly ecclesiastical books owned by priests or churches. For example, a presbyter had pawned "a book of mass" of the Church of Saint Savior, and another priest, who had "many books," left his breviary to the presbyter of the Church of Saint James of Višnjica in 1333. Still another priest and patrician in 1338 possessed a breviary, a volume of chants, and a missal. We have already spoken of books that Anthony of Montefiore had in Serbia in 1337. One more from among others in the fourteenth century was a nobleman from an outstanding family in Kotor, Thomas Pauli de Thoma. He had been accepted into the Ragusan patriciate and in 1329 left a legacy for a missal and a manual to be provided for his chapel to Saint Nicolas in Dubrovnik.

It is impossible to list here all the testaments, inventories, and other documents which show the presence of books, more numerous and important because of their quality and variety, in fifteenth-century Dubrovnik. Therefore, only a few examples will be given. In the previous chapter we commented about thirty books owned in 1418 by *"Doctor Magister Petrus physicus,"* son of Albertinus de Camurata. Another testament, again of a physician, "Master Jacobus de Prothonotariis, knight and medical doctor from Messina," who was killed in Serbia in 1439, listed thirteen books, including a breviary, a work by Seneca, and others. Religious books did not disappear from the interest of fifteenth-century Ragusans. Their testaments continued to have frequent mention of money left to buy books for churches and of breviaries left to priests; on the other hand, it is evident that priests themselves now possessed more than exclusively ecclesiastical books. For example, in 1464 a priest spoke of "all my books," and another, in the following year, mentioned "all my booklets." Interestingly, it seems that the priests did not hesitate to use their religious books for practical purposes which had little to do with religion or letters. This was the case in 1473 when "the venerable man, Lord Dominicus de Babalio, Canon of Dubrovnik" and a patrician, stated in his testament that he had pawned his new missal to another canon and patrician in order to obtain thirty hyperperi needed for a topcoat.

Priests and physicians, however, were not the only ones to own books and be interested in them. In 1478 there was mention of nineteen "big and small" books which had belonged to the late "Master George Spano, physician," but other persons possessed books as well. In 1462 the nobleman Matthew Djurdjević owned "books of statutes and laws of the land and a book written by my hand in which are entered the houses of noblemen and the dead noblemen and various other things." In 1464 the patrician Marin Restić left all his books to his grandson who was at the time studying in Padua. An interesting testament from Ston in 1500 mentioned a whole series of books, including works by Cicero, Suetonius, Ovid, Vergil, and others. There were many houses, both those of patricians and of rich citizens, in which books were kept and read. These were all manifestations of the spread of the new, humanistic spirit in Dubrovnik. Books were expensive luxuries, objects which frequently could be obtained only through the painstaking work of copying their texts by hand or having them copied by experts.

There were in Dubrovnik such experts, particularly among the priests, but the notaries and chancellors of the city seem to have been particularly active in arranging for books to be copied and even exported from Dubrovnik. In 1412 the priest Marin Kovačić promised to the Ragusan notary and chancellor Jacobus de Ugodonicis "to write with his own hand a beautiful, legal, and solemn missal" similar to the one the cathedral had but "with somewhat bigger letters." The pages were to be "white, good, square, and without any diminution at the corners." Kovačić was supposed to write in the book all the prayers used by Rugusans and others. He was "to form the big letters and all the other small letters well rounded and miniated in two good and excellent colors, that is to say, cinnabar and the fine overseas blue." The work was to be completed within eight months at a price of thirty-five ducats. Books were also exported from Dubrovnik. In 1429 a man from the island of Rab, living in Trogir, received from a Ragusan chancellor "a volume of thirty-two works by Seneca, written on parchment, and an explanation of Seneca's letters, on paper," to be carried to "Guido de Spilimbergo," who lived in Rijeka (Fiume). The fact that buying or copying books was a difficult and expensive business did not discourage the Ragusans, and this certainly speaks well for their cultural level at the time.

A most important date in connection with the role played by books in the cultural life of Dubrovnik was the year 1465. In February of that year the prominent astronomer, diplomat, bibliophile, and intellectual, Ivan Gazul, died. His testament dealt at length with his many books. Gazul bequeathed all his volumes pertaining to canon law and the holy scriptures to the Cathedral of Saint Mary the Major in Dubrovnik on the condition that they be put in one place, chosen by the procurators of the church, "where they must remain for perpetuity, as long as those books will last, for the convenience of those who would like to see or read something in the said books, and they cannot be given and accommodated to anybody in particular, but must always stay, as it was said, in a library [*in una biblioteca*] for the convenience of those who would like to read or see anything." Gazul ordered that his "other books" be disposed of by the executors of his testament. One of his volumes, however, was probably on loan to a priest who had to give it back. From the rest of the testament it is evident that Gazul expected his books, except those left to the library in the cathedral, to be sold and a number of his debts to be paid and legacies made from the profit.

Thus Gazul, in effect, created the first public library in Dubrovnik. The fact that he wanted his books to be kept in the cathedral is not surprising; not only was he a priest, but the cathedral in Dubrovnik, as in many other Western cities, was considered to be the safest place in town. By entrusting the cathedral with the preservation of his volumes, Gazul was simply following in the steps of the Ragusan government itself, which kept its documents, as well as its treasury, there. The books that Gazul left in 1465 laid down the foundation of the Scientific Library in Dubrovnik which exists to this day in the city. Others followed his example, particularly priests. Thus in October, 1473, the presbyter Nicolas Djončić, "*decretorum doctor*" and former principal of the Ragusan high school, in his testament left all his "legal books to the Church of Saint Mary the Major on the same condition under which the books of Johannes Gazulus were bequeathed." Djončić, however, had many other books and libels. He mentioned a writing of Saint Augustine's monologues, an old explication of the Gospel, and other writings—booklets in which there were treatises of canon law, letters, jokes, poetry. He kept the books in coffers. Some were to be sold; others were bequeathed to various priests. All the theological and philosophical volumes were to be given to the Dominican monastery and church, and some books were left to Andrew Kotruljević. The mention of the Dominican monastery is particularly significant, since both the Dominican and the Franciscan monasteries became very important centers for collecting manuscripts and books, and in a later period their libraries developed into repositories of the manuscripts of Ragusan literary men, keeping this role until the present time.

Indeed, beginning in the fifteenth century, Ragusan writers produced a series of literary works which show, better than anything else, the high quality of Dubrovnik's cultural achievements, but we shall not deal with this activity in greater detail, because it belongs mostly to the sixteenth century. In the fifteenth century there first were minor poems, written in Latin and on the model of the Italian humanistic poets. Some poets in Dubrovnik knew Greek and wrote verses in that language too. One of them, Djivo Gučetić, in the second half of the fifteenth century, is said to have written poems in Latin, Greek, and Slavic. In his testament he mentioned his "Greek and Latin books." Slavic, however, very quickly found its way in the new poetic activity. In fact, it seems very probable that there were Slavic poets from the earliest period of this cultural revival, but we know almost nothing of them. Even the first six lines of Slavic poetry, written in Cyrillic letters in the year 1421, were preserved only by chance on the margin of an archival book from the thirteenth century.

The first complete Slavic poems which have been preserved date from the second half of the fifteenth century. The two earliest known poets were Šiško Menčetić and Djore Držić. Both of them wrote the Slavic text in roman script, and they were very much influenced by Italian contemporary poetry. However, they introduced in their poetry many elements of Slavic folk poetry. This is one of the essential characteristics of the entire range of Ragusan literary work in the fifteenth century and later, of which the poems of Menčetić and Držić were only the precursors.

The literature of ancient Dubrovnik provides an excellent example of the role that city served as a link between the East and the West and of its capacity for absorbing influences from both sides, creating in turn its own original works. Even in the Latin products of Ragusan authors there are many Slavic folk elements. The same holds true for the literary works of Croatian writers in Dalmatia at the time. But perhaps the most striking achievements in this respect are the comedies of the famous Marin Držić in the sixteenth century. With exquisite sense and great talent, this Ragusan author blended purely Italian models and influences with genuine Slavic folk traditions, producing comedies in the Slavic language—notably *Uncle Maroje* and *The Miser*— whose originality and wit ensure their success on the stage to this day.

Another group of authors whose works do not belong exactly to the literary production but whose literary ambitions —at least with some of them—were not absent from their endeavors were the historiographers. Historiography appeared in Dubrovnik for the first time in the fourteenth century, and the first known author was John of Ravenna, Ragusan chancellor from 1384 to 1387. His work, called *Historia Ragusii*, a geographical description of Dubrovnik and its life, shows that the author was somewhat less than favorably impressed with the city at the time. Much more important is the excellent work of the already mentioned Philippus de Diversis, written in 1440. In *The Site of the Buildings, Policies, and Praiseworthy Habits of the Illustrious City of Ragusium*, de Diversis gave a comprehensive picture of the administrative, social, economic, and cultural situation in Dubrovnik in the first half of the fifteenth century, and, despite some critical remarks, it is clear that he was very favorably impressed. Toward the end of the fifteenth century an anonymous man, possibly a friar, wrote a book of annals of Dubrovnik up to 1485 to which a group of later authors added information until 1700. Furthermore, a Ragusan who had studied in Paris, Lodovicus Tubero Crijević, wrote his *Commentarii* in which he showed particular interest for Hungarian and Ottoman affairs. All of these works were written in Latin. In the second half of the sixteenth century, Nicolas Ranjina wrote in Italian the *Annali di Ragusa*, which covers the period until 1552. *Copioso ristretto degli annali di Rausa*, by Giacomo di Pietro Luccari (Lukarević), is a valuable work published in 1605 and covering Ragusan history until 1600. From a considerably later period, the end of the seventeenth and the first half of the eighteenth century, comes the best Ragusan historical work, the *Ragusan Chronicle*, written in Italian by Junius Restić and dealing with events up to 1451.

We should now cast a quick glance on the development of fine arts in Dubrovnik in the fourteenth and fifteenth centuries. First of all, a school of painting had its roots in Dubrovnik probably as far back as the eleventh century and achieved the pinnacle of its development in the fifteenth and sixteenth centuries. There is no doubt that this school had considerable importance in the cultural life of the city. The artists, who came to Dubrovnik from the Balkan hinterland, Dalmatia, Italy, and even Germany, brought with them their particular styles. Among them were families in which painting had been a tradition for generations. Multiple influences, particularly from Italy and from Byzantium, left their traces on the paintings produced in Dubrovnik, which for the most part show unique characteristics. These paintings, in turn, influenced the artistic production in the Balkan hinterland. The Ragusan government supported artistic endeavors in various ways.

Toward the end of the fifteenth and the beginning of the sixteenth century, two leading painters brought the Ragusan school of painting to the highest point of its development. They were Nicolas Božidarević and Mihoč Hamzić. Božidarević, son of a peasant painter, was educated in Venice. Although his works were greatly influenced by austere religious norms, they clearly showed an evolution toward Renaissance artistic concepts. Hamzić, descendant of a German family from Köln which had settled in Ston, studied some time with the famous Andrea Mantegna in Mantua. His paintings definitely belonged to the Renaissance style.

The Ragusan school of painting served as another intermediary in the exchange of influences between East and
West. Many painters took apprentices from the city itself
and from the nearby Balkan areas and thus transmitted
their knowledge and their style to new generations and to
local people. On the other hand, a number of Ragusan
painters undoubtedly worked in Italy and can probably be
designated by the general denomination *Schiavone*, given in
that country to many artists from the eastern Adriatic coast.
On the whole, the Ragusan school produced large numbers
of paintings in Dubrovnik, most of which were commissioned by churches or for them. Though many were destroyed in fires or in the terrible earthquake of 1667, a
number survive and can be seen today in churches and
museums in the city and its vicinity.

It is interesting that in a later period the Ragusan archbishop, Lodovico Beccadelli (1556–64), played a major role
in artistic contacts between Dubrovnik and the leading
Italian painters. He invited Michelangelo to visit Dubrovnik,
and it seems that the great artist was willing to go but was
prevented by the death of a companion. Beccadelli was also
in constant touch with Titian, who had painted his portrait.
It seems that the archbishop invited this illustrious artist to
visit Dubrovnik, but again without success. Nevertheless,
Dubrovnik's links with Titian and his school, as well as with
the Bellini brothers and their school, were rather strong.
Titian had already done a painting for a Ragusan patrician
in 1520, but this work never reached the city; it remained
in Ancona, where it is today. However, there were at least

three paintings by Titian in Dubrovnik itself, two of which still survive, as well as a number of works by minor Italian artists of the period.

There was little sculpture of excellence produced in Dubrovnik. The exceptions are few. There are, for example, the capitals of the columns in the Franciscan cloister—exquisite fourteenth-century works done by the artist Miho from Bar —and the Gothic portal of the Franciscan church. There also are the capitals of the Dominican cloister columns and the portal of that church, not as valuable as the Franciscan ones; capitals on columns in the houses and gardens of some patricians; and ornaments on both Onofrio's fountains and on the Sponza Palace. The most important sculptures, however, are those serving as ornaments on the Rector's Palace, dating from the fourteenth and fifteenth centuries. Most outstanding are the capitals of the columns of the façade of the palace and the ornaments of the main portal.

Hindering the development of sculpture in Dubrovnik was the refusal of the government to allow any representations of individuals by statues. It was only in the late sixteenth century that the erection of a bust of little artistic value to Miho Pracat, a rich merchant who had left all his properties to the state and who had performed great services for the republic, was approved, but even that one was erected inside the Rector's Palace, not in a public place. The only other human representation was the statue of Orlando, erected in 1417, a mediocre work by the sculptors Anthony of Dubrovnik and Bonino of Milan; of course, it was not a monument to a person but a symbol of communal freedom.

Recently a beautiful statue of an old man has been discovered and is considered to be the work of the prominent Croatian architect and sculptor, Juraj Dalmatinac.

It is noteworthy, however, that in spite of its weakness, sculpture also served as a link between the East and the West. In fact, there were Ragusan sculptors who went to Italy and worked there. One of them was Simeon Raguseus, a thirteenth-century artist whose name figures to this day on the portal of a church in Barletta, in southern Italy. On the other hand, several Italians played prominent roles in the shaping of Dubrovnik's sculpted ornaments. One was Petrus Martini from Milan, who worked on the sculptures of Onofrio's fountain, the Rector's Palace, and other objects. His fame was such that he was later invited to go to the court of King Alphons of Aragon, in Naples, from where he eventually went to the French royal court, with the high title of "royal sculptor."

Let us add briefly that wood carving was well known in Dubrovnik from the thirteenth century on and that, in the fourteenth and fifteenth centuries, this artistic activity produced elaborate frames which enhanced the beauty of Ragusan paintings, as well as fine ceilings and other objects. Wood-carved polychrome statues were also produced, and their quality was such that they were exported to southern Italy. The making of medallions was an art which made one Ragusan famous throughout the Mediterranean world. Pavko Antojević, after having been assistant to the outstanding Italian sculptor Donatello, made medallions for King Alphons of Naples. Then in the 1470's he lived and worked in the court of the Ottoman sultan Mohammed the Conqueror, a great promoter of the arts. Eventually Antojević returned to Dubrovnik and took part in making some sculptures on the Rector's Palace, at the same time also working as a goldsmith.

This brings us to gold- and silversmithing in Dubrovnik, an activity which flourished in the city in the fourteenth and fifteenth centuries. The silversmiths had a long tradition and became very numerous in Dubrovnik. Some of them were of foreign origin, Italian and other, but the majority at this time were domestic masters. With large quantities of Serbian and Bosnian silver readily available in Dubrovnik, they produced works of high quality for churches—plates, ornaments for relics, statues of saints, particularly Saint Blaise, and other objects—and for individuals. Patricians and rich merchants not only from Dubrovnik but from Venice, Milan, Ferrara, and other Italian cities ordered fine objects to be made for them by the Ragusan silversmiths. Very little, however, has been preserved.

An important aspect of silversmithing was the production of luxurious articles for the government, to be used as presents for visiting personalities and to be sent as gifts to rulers and feudal lords in Hungary, Naples, Serbia, Bosnia, and, later, to the Ottoman court. The Balkan rulers were interested in obtaining objects of precious metals produced by Ragusan craftsmen or imported through Dubrovnik. They sometimes even invited to their lands gold- and silversmiths from Dubrovnik or from Western Europe. It must be pointed out, however, that in the Balkan countries there existed a local production of silverware, and quite a few rulers and feudal lords were able to send products made by their silversmiths to

Dubrovnik or Venice in deposit or for other purposes. Thus in this field also there was an exchange of men and articles going in both directions, a clear indication of a mutual exchange of influences in which Dubrovnik almost inevitably played the role of intermediary.

Let us add that the people of Dubrovnik and the lords of the Balkan hinterland, by the first half of the fourteenth century, were interested in the glass products of Murano, in Italy, and in the fifteenth century glass production was started in Dubrovnik itself. Another field, that of music, was not unknown in Dubrovnik, although there is not much that can be said about it. The government employed trumpeters and other musicians for ceremonies and festivities. Some of these men came from Italy, others from Greece, and some were local men. What their role was outside of state ceremonies and festivities and what their influence was in the life of Dubrovnik are very hard to evaluate. Considering the length of time some of them stayed in the city, it may be assumed that they did influence the development of at least some musical interest among Ragusans.

When speaking of intellectual life and culture in Dubrovnik, it is necessary to consider briefly the position of the church because of its well-known influence in these areas. Dubrovnik was a Roman Catholic city, and its population was religious as much as the population in any other Western European, Catholic town. From Byzantine times, Dubrovnik always belonged to the sphere of ecclesiastical jurisdiction of the Roman pope and was an important clerical center, having become an archbishopric in 1022. Moreover, the Ragusan archbishopric was the religious center for a vast hinterland region which belonged largely to the Serbian state, and this situation lasted until the middle of the thirteenth century when Bar became the religious center of Catholics in Serbia. On the other hand, it was in the thirteenth century that the Serbian Orthodox Church, under the leadership of its first autocephalous archbishop, Rasto-Sava Nemanjić, began its expansion westward from a line running from Sirmium to Ras to Prizren which, roughly speaking, formed its frontier until then. The tendency was to make the frontier of the Serbian church coincide with the frontier of the newly created and rapidly expanding Serbian state.

These were not the only difficulties, however. The existence of a "Bosnian Church," considered by the Catholic clergy to be at least unorthodox, if not downright heretical, constituted another major problem for Dubrovnik in its dealings with the hinterland. This was particularly true in the fifteenth century, when Bosnian "Christians" became an important part of the Bosnian state hierarchy and when "heretical" leaders began appearing in Dubrovnik as envoys of powerful Bosnian personalities. Their benevolence was also important to Ragusans who went to Bosnia. The pragmatic Ragusans found a solution to the problem by viewing Bosnian "Christian" diplomats as political men and not religious figures, the same way they treated Orthodox Serbs.

To deal effectively with religious problems in foreign affairs, the Ragusans had to have a definite and clear ecclesiastical policy within their own state. Indeed, despite being good Catholics, they never allowed the church to impose its views, interests, or rules on the political life and activity of the city. Political decisions were an exclusive prerogative of the patricians, duly constituted in their three governmental councils. The church, the archbishop, and the clergy were respected, but their competence was consistently restricted to matters pertaining to the church, that is, to religious life. Through subtle—and sometimes not so subtle—controls, the Ragusan government saw to it that the church did not encroach beyond what was considered to be its rightful field of endeavor. This work alone, however, was more than sufficient to take all the time and energy of church officials.

There were scores of churches and monasteries in Dubrovnik and its vicinity. The first religious order to come to the area was the Benedictines, who founded their oldest monastery on the small island of Lokrum in 1023. The antiquity of the Benedictine presence, however, did not prevent the Ragusan government from acting very harshly toward the order when it considered that its interests were threatened by Benedictine behavior. Thus in 1494 the predominantly Italian monks of the monastery on Lokrum were threatened by the Ragusan government with expulsion within three days unless they accepted into the monastery a group of Ragusan patricians and other men as monks. This was just one instance of the general rule of Ragusan policy toward the church.

The Franciscans and the Dominicans arrived in Dubrovnik in the thirteenth century, soon after the orders were organized. They had several monasteries in Ragusan territory, but, of course, the most important were those inside the city itself (see Chapter III and above). Nunneries were especially numerous in Dubrovnik. The most interesting among them was the convent of Saint Clara, where daughters of patrician families from Dubrovnik and the nearby Slavic regions were accepted, sometimes at the age of fourteen or fifteen years. The conditions of life in this, as well as in other cloisters, were generally bad. The Ragusans did bequeath varying amounts of money to monasteries and churches, and the government helped them from time to time, but the situation inside the monastic walls was far from satisfactory, particularly from the hygienic, and sometimes even moral, point of view. Some scandals which broke out, involving nuns, monks, or priests, created considerable trouble and difficulty for Ragusan secular, as well as ecclesiastical, authorities.

In order to keep ecclesiastical personalities from playing a role in political life and to keep individual patricians from obtaining too much influence and prestige, the Ragusans decided in 1360 to oppose any future appointment by the pope of a Ragusan as archbishop of the city. In that year Elias de Saraca (Ilija Saračić), a Ragusan patrician who had been archbishop of Dubrovnik for eighteen years, died. Saračić in his younger days had lived in Rome, Avignon, and Bologna and in 1342 was appointed—contrary to the desire of the Ragusans—archbishop of the city. In that position Saračić achieved great prestige among the Ragusans and took a very active part in politics. He was, indeed, one of the key figures in the important political events of 1357 and 1358 and was the head of the Ragusan mission which stipulated Dubrovnik's acceptance of Hungarian protection in 1358. Fortunately for Dubrovnik, this able and influential man was a great patriot, thoroughly dedicated to Dubrovnik's freedom and political independence. Nevertheless, after his death the Ragusans did not want to take any new risks and so thwarted all future ambitions of their citizens to become archbishop.

As noted earlier, Dubrovnik confronted problems originating from the expansion of Serbia and its Orthodox ecclesiastical organization in regions near Dubrovnik and in its trade area. Nor could the increasing influence of the Bosnian Church be forgotten. Another major concern was how to treat the Orthodox populations from the hinterland when they came to Catholic Dubrovnik, as they did constantly and in large numbers. Individuals of Orthodox faith could not become permanent citizens of Dubrovnik unless they accepted Catholicism. Such a regulation was prescribed not out of religious fanaticism but because the Ragusan government wanted to have a religiously homogeneous population in its territory. However, there were times when Dubrovnik had to tolerate the existence of Orthodox enclaves even on its own land. Such a situation prevailed on the peninsula of Pelješac after 1333, when Dušan, in selling the territory to Dubrovnik, stipulated "that a Serbian priest live and chant in the churches which are in Ston and on Rt [Pelješac]." Similarly, Orthodox religious elements were preserved in the region of Konavli after it came into Ragusan hands. In both regions the population was Orthodox, but gradually, taking care not to offend the Serbs or Bosnians, the Ragusans managed to catholicize these lands.

On the other hand, while people of Orthodox faith could not obtain permanent residence in the city, they were allowed to come and go freely, whether as merchants or as servants or in other capacities. Many servants, of course, became Catholics, but this was done *via facti*, through their long stay in Dubrovnik, rather than through enforcement. The Ragusans, however, did not allow the building of an Orthodox church in their city at this time. The only exception was in 1434, when they admitted the possibility of building an Orthodox church for the Bosnian duke Sandalj Hranić if the pope gave them permission, but this plan was never carried out. The reluctance of the Ragusans to have an Orthodox church inside their city was not caused by any hatred of the Orthodox population, but simply was part of their policy of religious homogeneity.

This policy, together with the preservation of strict political independence from the Catholic hierarchy and the control of the Catholic Church in Dubrovnik itself, was absolutely necessary for the city to survive in its special and precarious position at the edge of two worlds, the Catholic in the West and the Orthodox in the East. The arrival of the Islamic, Ottoman state on Ragusan borders in the second half of the fifteenth century did nothing to ease the situation. It is not surprising, therefore, that Dubrovnik constantly and carefully balanced its measures in order to preserve its independence from all sides. Because of this need to calculate every step and to keep religious influences in check, the role of the Catholic Church in Dubrovnik's cultural life was not conspicuous. Although paintings were made for churches, as well as sculptures and silverware, and there was poetry inspired by religious motives, the church was not in a position to exert pressure or effective control on intellectual activities as a whole.

In summary it can be said that in the fourteenth and fifteenth centuries Dubrovnik initiated intellectual and artistic endeavors in many fields. The city became the principal center of culture among the southern Slavs until the nineteenth century and one of the very important focuses of all the Slavic lands, as well as of the Mediterranean world. At a time when Croatia submitted to Hungarian domination from the beginning of the twelfth century, and when Serbia and Bosnia were suffering Ottoman occupation from the middle of the fifteenth century, Dubrovnik was expressing its creativity in freedom and producing extremely valuable works.

Many of the elements in this production came from the Slavic ethnic world, but others arose from the Italian, humanistic culture in the West. Thus in its intellectual and artistic endeavors, as in other fields, Dubrovnik once again acted as a vital link between the two areas and as a middleman in the mutual exchange of their cultures.

VI

Everyday Life in Dubrovnik

In the bustling city of Dubrovnik, with its mild climate and many sunny days, life was greatly concentrated in the streets and squares, as well as in the busy harbor. This was and still is a general Mediterranean pattern. In the thirteenth and fourteenth centuries, when Dubrovnik was smaller, when its activities were still in a stage of development and its streets were still unpaved and surrounded mainly by wooden houses, it was not very pleasant to walk or work in the streets. But in the fifteenth century, with streets and squares paved, with drainage and sewage systems organized, with garbage regularly removed, and, above all, with bigger and more beautiful stone houses, churches, and palaces, Dubrovnik became a city whose streets offered a fascinating spectacle of life.

Because of its peculiar geographic position and the resulting close relations with both the East and the West, the city became the meeting place of men from different parts of the Mediterranean world. Men from Italy and other Western countries, from the Balkans or from the Levant mixed with local people in the streets and squares, went about their business in shops and in the harbor, and traveled in caravans to and from the city. Ships from Dalmatia, Italy, Greece, Sicily, and even France and Spain sailed into the harbor. In fact, the rush was sometimes so great that ships that were unable to enter the harbor immediately had to wait in line in a bay of the small nearby island of Lokrum.

In Dubrovnik's streets and squares, in its taverns and hostelries, all languages were spoken. The Dalmatian Croats and the Serbians and Bosnians from the hinterland spoke the Slavic language that the Ragusan population itself was using, and so there was no communication problem. The Italians found no difficulty either, for their language was the commercial language of the Mediterranean, known to many Ragusans. It was certainly more difficult for Hungarians, Greeks, Spaniards, Germans, and Frenchmen, but for them, too, Italian probably served as a general means of communication. Later, when the Ottomans became neighbors and started arriving in Dubrovnik in increasing numbers, language did not present great difficulties, because most Ottomans were of Slavic origin, from the Balkan hinterland, and were fluent in the Slavic language.

The arrival and departure of ships was always an event of interest, not only to the merchants, captains, and sailors directly involved but also to the population as a whole. Every Ragusan ship, because of its crew members and their families, the goods it was carrying, and the investors, was of great interest to more than the few men directly involved in its navigation. Foreign ships, on the other hand, interested the populace not only because of the goods they brought or took away but also because of the income that their crews brought to taverns and other places in the city. There was always a natural element of curiosity which stimulated many people to spend their time in the harbor even though they had little to do there, thus adding to its picturesque and dynamic traffic. The arrival and departure of caravans toward the Balkan hinterland were events of similar interest to the Ragusans.

The government had a special concern in the movement of merchants, ships, and caravans. It was not only the collecting of customs fees, which necessitated constant vigilance by officials in the harbor, the customs house, and elsewhere. Nor was it health control only. The collection of information on lands from which ships or caravans came interested the government very much. Every Ragusan merchant was expected, if asked, to report to the government everything he knew of the lands he visited or through which he traveled or any rumors that he might have heard about other regions. To do so was a patriotic duty, not a spy activity, and in many instances merchants, captains, and others gave information to the government spontaneously if they considered it important to the state. On the other hand, the government did not hesitate to ask for such information, even from foreigners in the city, if it believed that vital interests of Dubrovnik were involved.

Much news and information were exchanged in the Loggia, a square building of red and white stone which was near the Rector's Palace and the Church of Saint Blaise. Sitting on benches under the arcades of this building—which does not exist any more—merchants and captains, craftsmen and sailors, patricians and commoners, people of all kinds, local and foreign, arriving from various parts of the Balkans and the Mediterranean, talked about their experiences, exchanged local gossip, and played chess or gambled. (These games sometimes were played even in the cathedral, which periodically provoked strict prohibitions by the government.) Thus the Loggia was an important center for gathering information, but the government did not hesitate, when circumstances required, to forbid the spreading of information on some particular subject, both orally and in writing.

Because of the information brought to the city by merchants and other persons and also through the letters of Ragusan ambassadors, merchants, and others—constantly written to the government from many parts of the Balkans, Italy, the Levant, and other places—Dubrovnik became one of the most important centers of political information in Europe in the fifteenth century and later. The government was greatly helped in its decision-making by the excellent intelligence it received from the Ottoman and Byzantine courts, from Serbia, Bosnia, Croatia, and Hungary, from Venice, Rome, and the whole of Italy, from France, Spain, and even Germany and England. At the same time, many of these powers profited by the knowledge they were able to acquire in Dubrovnik. There can be no doubt that, once the Ottoman Empire settled on the whole of the Balkans and Dubrovnik became the only free state on the edge of the Ottoman world, the city also became a most valuable center of information on the Ottomans for the whole Christian, Western world and presumably a very important source of information on that world for the Ottomans.

The picturesque character of the streets and squares of

Dubrovnik was enhanced by the costumes people wore. Before the development of domestic textile production, the local inhabitants depended for their clothing on imports of woven materials, mainly from Venice and through it from farther west. Certain amounts of simpler, rough textiles came from the Balkan interior or were locally produced. Those imported from Italy were generally of a superior quality— silk, scarlet, brocade, velvet—but fustian and simpler textiles from Flanders (often called Ypria) also were imported through Italy. All of these textiles were frequently exported from Dubrovnik into Serbia and Bosnia. Some French and British textiles, small quantities of Byzantine luxury textiles or cloth embroidered in Greek style, as well as a variety of eastern materials, called Tartar tissues, were also imported. Of course, not all of these textiles were used for clothing. Many served as curtains, tablecloths, bedspreads, ornaments, and such. In the 1420's a domestic production of textiles was started and grew rapidly in Dubrovnik (see Chapter III), providing its inhabitants with an increased opportunity to have better clothing.

With the imports and later the domestic production, it was possible for the inhabitants of Dubrovnik to dress adequately. Indeed, in this city, as elsewhere in Western cities, the patrician costumes were different from those of ordinary citizens. Although the garments of all of them had similarities with other European garments, they also had local characteristics. John of Ravenna in the 1380's considered the way Ragusans dressed to be strange and funny. It is known that the ordinary Ragusan citizens at this time used parts of Slavic garb and the Slavic names for them: for example, a form of shoes, called *opanke*, known and used under the same name to this day in the Balkans, and a sort of Slavic stockings with garters, *podvezače*. However, Ragusan costumes in time increasingly came to resemble those in the West. The resemblance was enhanced by the presence and work of Western tailors in Dubrovnik. In 1421 a tailor from Savoy, another from Britain, and a third from Brabant, and a fourth from Zadar opened a shop in Dubrovnik, having formed a society for four years.

De Diversis in 1440 described feminine garb, mentioning that virgins wore a silver gilded crown adorned with jewels on their heads. Another text from the end of the same century does not speak of that item, but emphasizes that the feminine costume "is more than honest," covering the body up to the throat. It seems that at this time the Ragusans dressed much like the Venetians, although retaining some small details of Slavic or, later, Turkish garb. Generally the garments worn by the patricians preserved fewer Slavic elements than the costumes of the citizenry and, of course, the peasants. Among the peasants, Slavic clothes remained very much in use until recent times. On the whole, it is possible to say that the varied clothing of the local people, together with the great diversity of garbs worn by the many foreigners coming from every part of the Mediterranean and European world, created a lively and ever-changing picture on the sunny streets of Dubrovnik.

An important part of the costume was jewelry. It was worn mainly by women, although men also owned and were greatly interested in jewelry because of its value in business, as pawns and such. Jewelry was a luxury article which was harder to get in early times, but as soon as the Serbian and later the Bosnian silver mines opened, jewelry became an important object of dress and trade. To give just a few examples, as early as 1282 a woman in her testament mentioned her gold adornments, while another had "three pairs of gilded silver earrings with chains." A man in 1325 had two silver belts, and another mentioned among the belongings of his wife three pairs of gilded silver earrings and three pairs of gold ones. He also had two silver belts as pawns. In 1377 a Ragusan had a large number of gold and silver jewels and other objects as pawns from various people. In the fifteenth century the number of luxury objects and personal jewels increased with the prosperity of the city.

The Ragusan government, however, was not happy about the growth of luxury and the greed for gold and silver in the city. From the thirteenth century on, it issued stern orders from time to time to limit the right of its citizens to possess jewels, regulate luxurious dressing among women, and curb the tendency toward excessive dowries, expensive marriages, and other too fatuous festivities. But this should not lead us to the conclusion that life was dull or that egalitarianism prevailed in Dubrovnik. As usual, these kinds of measures had only limited success. The best proof is the constant repetition of such decrees and their increasing severity, particularly at the beginning of the sixteenth century when they were extended to include even men's robes and behavior.

In spite of the intensity of life in the streets and squares, there is no doubt that the home was a most important part of life for the Ragusans. Houses varied greatly, of course, depending on who owned them, patricians or poor people, and also depending on the period. In the fourteenth century, the predominantly wooden houses frequently had only one room on each of the two, three, or four floors, with corresponding numbers of wooden staircases. In bigger houses there was usually a hall on the second floor, used for festivities and sometimes for everyday work. On the upper floors there were built-in wooden wardrobes, sometimes with shelves inside. The kitchen was in some instances built as an addition to the house, with its own roof. Ordinarily, however, the kitchen was either on the first floor, with an adjacent small dining room, or on the top floor. Inside the kitchen there was a tile or stone fireplace with a funnel-shaped chimney. There was also a stone basin, and very frequently the toilet was built inside, separated from the rest of the kitchen by an enclosure resembling a wooden wardrobe. Sometimes the toilet was located in a wooden addition to the outer wall of the uppermost floor of the house, but, since this was un-hygienic, the government tried to abolish it.

In big halls were benches which sometimes also served as beds. Beds were known in Dubrovnik as early as the thir-teenth century and perhaps earlier, but not all houses had them then or even later. Where they were to be found, they were not numerous, even in large houses. The biggest known number of beds in a single house was three. They were tall, large, wooden structures, placed in separate rooms, and sev-eral persons could sleep on each one. Sometimes beds, at least on one side, were adjacent to the wall and attached to it. Around the bed or at the foot there were usually coffers in which bedding and other linens were kept. These coffers also served as steps to the bed and, in rich houses, were beautifully decorated with paintings. As for bedding, by the fourteenth century pillows, sheets, and blankets were known in Dubrovnik, but their quantities were small, even in the households of wealthy patricians. The largest known number of sheets in a household was six, which would indicate that they were probably seldom used and that people slept mostly in their clothes. Mattresses seem to have been filled with straw, feathers, or cotton.

In the fifteenth century, although the houses were bigger and built of stone, the basic plans did not change much, but documents concerning housebuilding show that the owners wanted to have more comfortable and better-decorated homes. Better-quality stone was used, and windows and doors were more elaborate. In the beginning of the century, "cages" above beds were mentioned, and the beds were surrounded by a sort of wooden enclosure or by nets to form an alcove. Later, "cages" were not found, but there was frequent mention of wooden caissons on ceilings, painted and sometimes richly decorated with figures, stars, and such. Beds acquired colored curtains and, in addition, there were tables, benches, and wardrobes in sleeping rooms. A new element in the fifteenth-century Ragusan home was the closet, and sometimes there were several of them in one house.

Another more interesting addition was the "studio." Most probably this was a writing desk and its immediate surroundings inside a room, sometimes near the bed. There were homes which had several studios in different parts of the house, each enclosed by decorated wooden panels which contained shelves. The existence of studios in later fifteenth-century Ragusan houses is certainly an indication of and the result of a greater interest in books and writing (see Chapter V). During the sixteenth century, with the increased wealth of the Ragusans, many improvements on house interiors and exteriors were made, but basically the homes remained unchanged. Perhaps the two most significant improvements were increases in the number of bedrooms and in the number of stone stoves in various rooms.

It is impossible to list here all the items a household possessed and used. On the whole, it is correct to say that in the fourteenth century household objects were simple and not too numerous. This simplicity was in tune with the houses and the city itself. This does not mean, however, that there were no luxury objects at all. Silverware especially was to be found, due to the intensive silver trade carried on between Dubrovnik and the Serbian and Bosnian mines. For example, in 1324 a Ragusan listed, among other possessions, six silver plates and a cup. In the fifteenth century such cases were more frequent and the lists were considerably longer. Household goods, in general, became more elaborate and numerous and included pictures on the walls. All of this, however, applied only to the rich or at least to the well-to-do, while the poor people continued to live much more modestly, not only in regard to their household possessions but their houses as well.

What were the people living in the houses of Dubrovnik like? It is, of course, very difficult to understand fully the mentality of the Ragusans, which certainly varied with the social and economic position of individuals and families. The patricians, after having taken exclusive political power into their hands, were, no doubt, very much aware of their special place and role. Their dedication to duty toward the state can only be commended, and their diplomatic ability and their stamina in meeting difficulties can only be admired. Partly because of these qualities, Dubrovnik survived as a free state for so long. This does not mean that the patricians did not have human vices, weaknesses, and desires, like any other men. Although it is very difficult to prove, there can be no doubt that in political deliberations there frequently were intrigue and faction fighting for power and influence.

The acquisition of wealth was a preoccupation of the patricians, since many of them, even members of influential old families, were far from being rich. The main source of wealth, moreover, was not state office, but trade. This can be seen very well in two fifteenth-century texts. De Diversis wrote in 1440 that, because of the poverty of Ragusan land and the large population, trade was the only source of prosperity; patrician fathers from earliest days educated their sons in this business, for they saw "in wealth happiness and every virtue in its acquisition and assiduous accumulation." Marin Gundulić, member of one of the greatest patrician families, wrote in his will in 1462: "I have been a nobleman of Dubrovnik and have had a big and demanding family, and wanting to avoid being put into the misery of living off public offices, I labored with the industry of the commerce so that my sons, too, could take my example in some activity and exercise the said commerce, by means of which they will be able to rise to some honor and prosperity."

Thus it is not an exaggeration to say that in each patrician there was a twofold personality: the politician and the merchant. As de Diversis said, "The care and the office of these noblemen, beyond commerce, is to govern, to augment, and to preserve the city." This was reflected in their whole way of life. Although the house of a patrician did not differ much from that of a correspondingly rich merchant, his daily activities were considerably different. A patrician, upon leaving his family and house, might visit his shop or attend the arrival of his ship or of his merchandise brought by other ships or caravans—all things that other merchants did too. But the patrician was required, in addition, to sit in the Major Council whenever it convened. If he was a senator, he had to attend frequent meetings of this important body. Finally, if he was a member of the Minor Council, he participated in the daily routine of governing the city. A patrician was expected not only to attend meetings, but to take part in discussions and to vote. These activities took a good deal of his time and energy. In addition, if a patrician was elected for a diplomatic mission, even a difficult one, he had to accept it, regardless of loss of time and money. On the other hand, as a merchant, he had to meet partners, to make decisions about credits, investments, ships, caravans, and so forth, and to keep track of what was going on in the Ragusan market and wherever else he had interests.

Merchants who were not patricians did not have their time taken up by political duties and offices. Their day could be entirely dedicated to their business. However, for both groups of merchants, the most burdensome and important part of business dealings was the trips that they had to make to nearby and faraway lands. It was not very difficult to go to Dalmatia, Kotor, or hinterland areas close to Dubrovnik, and such trips did not take too much time. But to go to Venice, southern Italy, Albania, or more remote Balkan regions was far from simple and much more time-consuming. Finally, a trip to Greece, Egypt, Syria, the Black Sea area, Sicily, Tunisia, Spain, Hungary, or Bosnian and Serbian localities in the rugged Balkan mountains required extensive preparations, lasted for months, and could be dangerous and very exhausting.

The position of women in Dubrovnik was not much different from the position women occupied elsewhere in the Western world at the time. There were some women whose work took them out of their homes. For example, almost all of the taverns selling wine in Dubrovnik were managed by women. Some women were engaged in business dealings too. One of the most prominent businesswomen in the middle of the fourteenth century was Philippa Menčetić, of a large and rich patrician family, who after her husband's death carried on his enterprises and became one of the wealthiest and most influential persons in the city. However, it might be argued that the greatest contribution of women was not in what they actually did in business and in other activities, but rather in the patient, constant support they offered their husbands, fathers, and brothers in their work. It took much perseverance, strength, and self-control for the women to put up with their men's long absences, with their constant preoccupation with politics and business, and with the usually numerous children, whose lives and education depended very heavily on the direction of their mothers. It can be said that in Dubrovnik, as in Venice, women were largely responsible for the city's greatness and its achievements through the unobtrusive and quiet support they gave to the men of the city in their endeavors.

Not all the women in Dubrovnik, however, were of this kind. Dubrovnik had its share of prostitution and similar problems. Prostitutes and concubines were mentioned in documents by the end of the thirteenth and the beginning of the fourteenth centuries. It seems that in early years prostitutes lived in a house in the old part of the city. This house was euphemistically called "the little castle," the women were frequently called "sinners," and the lady of the house had the unofficial and rather peculiar title of "abbess of the sinners." At the beginning of the fifteenth century, prostitutes were confined to a quarter inside the city near the seaside walls. However, there were always abuses of these rules and instances when "bad women" were accepted into private houses where they carried on their activities. In 1464 the government decided to expel a widow from Dubrovnik for a year for corrupting young men by bringing them to her home and entertaining them in such a way that they performed the "bad arts." Punishment for prostitutes could be very harsh. In 1495 a woman living in the center of Dubrovnik was arrested "for bad fame and corrupt life." Her punishment was to be tied to a chariot for a whole day, driven around the city and whipped, after which she was expelled forever from the city.

Prostitution in Dubrovnik, however, was only one sexual problem with which the government had to deal, and probably the easier one. It was much more difficult to handle the matter of concubines, who were frequently mistresses of patricians and sometimes lived in their houses. Moreover, many Ragusan patrician families systematically brought young female servants to their homes in the city from their estates in nearby areas, primarily from the region of Konavli, south of Dubrovnik, where women were considered particularly beautiful. These young girls served not only as servants but also as sexual partners for younger males in the family, who thus avoided visiting prostitutes and risking disease. The young girls, after a while, were presented in marriage by their masters to peasants, small craftsmen, or others of a corresponding social status, and the patrician family took care to provide the girl with a dowry and sometimes to help the prospective husband improve his economic situation. Some girls, on the other hand, never married but remained servants and in time became almost part of the family. Of course, not all the servants were so loyal, and there were many instances of girl servants bringing men into their masters' homes and helping them to steal, or escaping from their masters, for which prosecutions and punishments were very severe (cutting off the nose, for example).

The relationship between a young patrician and a young girl servant in his home became more complicated when a child was born as a result of their liaison. The young men usually recognized their paternity, but the child, being illegitimate, could have no claim to nobility or membership in the family. However, the family generally cared for the child by helping the mother (even arranging a convenient marriage and acceptance of the child) and later by helping the child obtain an education, get started on a job, and so forth. Fathers very frequently mentioned such children in their testaments. Besides, as already explained (see Chapter IV), from 1432 on, there was an orphanage in Dubrovnik where illegitimate children could find shelter. It should be added here that many Ragusans who lived for protracted periods of time in various places in the Balkan hinterland had mistresses there and, frequently, children with them. These women and children were not forgotten in testaments either.

There can be no doubt that prostitution, concubinage, and other forms of illegal sex life in Dubrovnik in the fourteenth and fifteenth centuries not only existed but increased with the growth in prosperity and with the increase in the numbers of sailors, merchants, craftsmen, and others going through the city or settling there. Even the "holy" pilgrims on their journey to Jerusalem did not disdain a visit to a Ragusan brothel. Of course, all of this does not mean that Dubrovnik was a haven for sexual enjoyment. It was neither more nor less "developed" in this respect than many other Western cities of its size, and it certainly could not compete with a metropolis such as Venice or Florence.

On the other hand, Dubrovnik did have a number of problems with its youth, as did other developed Western cities. Young men, particularly at night, behaved in the streets and squares of Dubrovnik in ways which were far from pleasing to their elders, and this situation continued for decades and centuries. It is true that the circulation at night was limited. After a certain hour people withdrew into their homes or into taverns, while the *capitaneus noctis,* "captain of the night," with his escort patrolled the city, punishing everybody whom he found walking around without a light. Nevertheless, young men, alone or in gangs, roamed the streets and, under dark arcades and vaults, in house gates and in narrow passages, fought battles among themselves. They also attacked passersby and, in particular, molested women. Fistfights and pulling of beards were almost daily occurrences, but there were more serious troubles: wounding with knives, clubbing with heavy sticks, and even murders. These were primarily the doing of young patricians and not always in the night. In April, 1493, a patrician murdered another "in the most elect and noble place of the city of Ragusium, in Placa." The killer was condemned to death but managed to escape.

There were also scenes of secret love in the dark of the vaults and arcades, and gangs of young men roamed around and sang obscene songs. In 1464, for example, eleven "young noblemen roamed the city at night singing some songs with most dishonest words" and "saying stupidities." "Dishonest words," however, were used most frequently in everyday quarrels between men or women, and they were mostly Slavic words, as quoted in judicial documents preserved in the Ragusan archives (see Chapter V).

Dubrovnik, because of its geographic location, was an important point on the route of pilgrims to Palestine. The story of Richard the Lion-Hearted shows this was true as early as the twelfth century (see Chapter III), and there are many documents illustrating this role of Dubrovnik from that time on. Among the pilgrims were all sorts of people from various Western countries, from Italy, France, England, Ireland, Germany, Hungary, and Bohemia, and so forth. According to Ragusan chroniclers, Saint Francis also visited Dubrovnik in 1219 on his journey to Palestine. Many Ragusans themselves made pilgrimages or bequeathed money in their testaments for priests or other persons to go to various shrines. These pilgrimages included journeys to Palestine, to churches in southern and central Italy, and, particularly in the fifteenth century, very frequently to Saint James of Compostella in Spain. Thus pilgrims and pilgrimages contributed to the general movement of men and, to an unknown degree, to the exchange of ideas and influences between Dubrovnik and various parts of the Mediterranean world.

In spite of the piety shown in preoccupation with pilgrimages and in many other ways, Ragusans in some walks of life could be very cruel and merciless. This was especially true in the way the problem of slavery was treated both before and after the partial abolition of the trade in Dubrovnik in 1416. Two examples, one from before and the other after the 1416 measure, will illustrate. In 1282 in the Ragusan court the abbot of the Church of Saint Andrew on the island of Šipan asserted that a woman named Dabrena and her son Paul were still slaves of his church, defending his claim on the grounds that Dabrena's mother, Desica, had formerly been the church's slave. During the presentation of his case the abbot introduced a notarial act from 1219 to prove his assertion. The defendants organized their defense around the argument that Dabrena was not Desica's daughter and consequently not a slave. Finally the court freed Dabrena and her son, but the case shows very clearly how persistently the concept of slavery remained in peoples' minds and that the more than sixty years which had elapsed between 1219 and 1282 made little difference in the validity of the demand.

The other, somewhat similar case is from 1430. A man

from nearby Trebinje demanded that a certain Pribitko be made his slave by the Ragusan court, because Pribitko was born to a slave of the petitioner. Pribitko admitted having been born to a slave, but asserted that the woman had been set free by the petitioner's father. However, he did not have any proof, and the man from Trebinje denied the assertion. The Ragusan court decided, therefore, that Pribitko must be a slave of the petitioner and follow him wherever he went.

With all the elements in favor of relatively better living conditions in Dubrovnik than in many other places (see Chapters III and IV), there nevertheless were unpleasant occurrences which disturbed life in the city. Fires were common events which caused great damage to Dubrovnik and its inhabitants. Although their number and extent decreased considerably in the fifteenth century, after the city became almost exclusively stone built and the streets were paved, they still posed an ever present threat to the lives and property of Ragusans. Another very distressing aspect of life in Dubrovnik was the constant menace of earthquakes, frequent because Dubrovnik was located in a particularly active earthquake zone. The chronicles relate many minor and major earthquakes throughout centuries, and there are notes, written by idle scribes on the margins of some archival books, telling of fires, earthquakes, and other catastrophes. There was nothing that could be done to protect against earthquakes, and the city suffered several major destructions, the worst of which occurred in 1667 (see Conclusion).

Attacks on the city by enemies from the outside were rather infrequent, because Dubrovnik was usually able through diplomacy and money to avert most onslaughts and open hostilities. There were nevertheless several attacks on Dubrovnik, either by land or sea. At such times the government took emergency measures to defend the city, and everybody was expected to obey orders and to perform his duty without hesitation. The measures included manning the walls, guarding the city gates, patrolling the streets, watching from high points for enemy ships, destroying houses outside the walls, rationing food and controlling its distribution, and so forth. In some instances ships were armed for naval defense, and men were recruited from nearby islands and regions of the republic. Patricians were in charge of the execution of such orders and measures, but prominent commoners also played important roles.

Life in Dubrovnik had its pleasant moments too. Hunting with falcons or dogs, horse racing, and target shooting were rather common forms of entertainment for both patricians and other citizens. Even today a small esplanade close to but outside the western gate to the city is called Brsalje, from *bersaglio*, "the mark," preserving in its name the memory of the times when it served as a shooting ground for the ancient Ragusans. For amusement indoors, masquerading became a popular way of spending long winter evenings, although the government was not always happy with what took place on such occasions and frequently forbade masquerading indoors as well as outdoors. Theatrical performances became more popular as entertainment only in the sixteenth century and then mainly for patrician families.

For the populace a fine occasion for amusement was the visit of a foreign dignitary to Dubrovnik. These visits, depending on the importance of the visitor and his relation to

Dubrovnik, were accompanied by a display of pageantry and various feasts. Prominent visitors were numerous in Dubrovnik in the fourteenth and fifteenth centuries, ranking from ambassadors and pilgrims to princes and rulers. Certainly the two most prestigious were the emperor of Serbia, Stephen Dušan, and the king of Hungary and Croatia, Sigismund of Luxembourg. Dušan arrived in the city with his wife and son and a large escort in 1350 on two Ragusan ships from Cavtat and was greeted in the harbor by the count and the whole nobility of Dubrovnik, probably with their wives. From there they went in a procession to the Rector's Palace, where Dušan stayed for three, possibly eight, days. The same ceremonies took place when he left. He was given luxurious presents, and the chroniclers say that he visited the Church of Saint Blaise—under construction at the time—as well as some other churches and gave them rich presents. The chronicles contain other information that is impossible to verify but which seems credible in view of other visits for which there is documentary evidence. Dušan, they say, was feted with constant banquets, amusements, and dances in the palace, and the palace itself was richly decorated with paintings done by "Greek painters" especially for this occasion and illustrating the emperor's many victories.

King Sigismund of Hungary and Croatia visited Dubrovnik for eight days at Christmas time in 1396, after his defeat at Varna. He, too, was solemnly received, housed in the Rector's Palace and treated with great respect. Sometimes, however, visits by prominent foreigners were less than a pleasure for the Ragusan government. For example, when Pietro Soderini, the president (*Gonfaloniere*) of the Florentine Republic, took refuge in Dubrovnik after he was over-thrown in 1512 by the Medicis, the government was considerably embarrassed. Soderini spent seven months not in the city but in a palace several miles to the northwest, on the coast, and the Ragusans, in spite of the difficulties he caused them, gave him full asylum and protection.

Religious festivities were another occasion for popular entertainment, with processions, dances in public squares, and so forth. This was particularly true of the feast day of Saint Blaise, the city's patron, celebrated on February 3. The ceremonies began on February 2 and continued through the next day, culminating in a procession and popular festivities and dances. This celebration attracted large numbers of people from the territory of the whole Republic of Dubrovnik, and a special remission of debts was given by the government for a week's time to enable Ragusans who stayed out of their state because of debts to come to the city for the occasion. The festivity, although connected to a religious occasion, had a very strong accent on symbolizing the freedom and independence of Dubrovnik and, because of its popular character, was a very picturesque, joyous, and noisy occasion, particularly after firearms became part of the celebration.

We have touched very briefly upon many aspects of Dubrovnik's life. Much could be added to this commentary, but on the whole it seems reasonable to conclude that life in Dubrovnik was similar to that in a number of other Western European cities at the time, although Dubrovnik had some advantages. Its pleasant climate and the concern of its government for sanitation, as well as the increasing prosperity of the city, certainly made living there somewhat easier than in many other places. In the various facets of the city's life, a blend of the East and the West could be felt, which gave Dubrovnik a unique flavor of Western civilization spiced with Eastern elements and influences.

Conclusion

D URING the fourteenth and fifteenth centuries, Dubrovnik evolved from a small, wooden city, dependent on Venice, into a territorially small, but economically strong and politically independent republic and a relatively large and comfortable stone-built and fortified city. The key to this development lay in Dubrovnik's role as middleman in trade carried on between the East—the Balkans—and the West—principally Italy—which brought great prosperity to the city. Forming a vital link between them and absorbing elements from both, it created a distinct civilization of its own. In all these respects, the two centuries that have been discussed here were of decisive importance to Dubrovnik and its future development.

The sixteenth century became the peak period of Dubrovnik's activity and progress. Its merchants were busily at work throughout the immense Ottoman Empire, where security and territorial unity, replacing previously existing state frontiers and arbitrary customs barriers imposed by local feudal lords, resulted in a considerable upsurge in trade and movement of persons. The Ottomans tolerated the Ragusans in their lands not only because the Ragusans had already been present for a long time and because they paid a tribute to the sultan, but also because the Ottomans, no doubt, were aware of the important role that Ragusan merchants played in the economy of their Balkan lands. Moreover, Dubrovnik itself was in a convenient location from which the Ottomans could keep an eye on the Western, Christian world.

Dubrovnik was, indeed, closely connected with the Western world, especially with Spain, which became the chief protector of the Ragusans in the West in the sixteenth century. Many Ragusan ships, considerably larger in size after the middle of the fifteenth century, visited Spanish ports and ventured in growing numbers toward England, Flanders, and other, more remote areas. In the sixteenth century Dubrovnik's commercial fleet sometimes included 180 ships and was one of the largest on the Mediterranean. It was also at this time that the first Ragusan ships made trips to the American continent.

Decline set in slowly toward the end of the sixteenth century. There were many reasons, and the discovery of America was only a minor one. More important was the rise of big Western European fleets on the Mediterranean, creating competition that was hard for Dubrovnik to withstand. The decisive element, however, was the decline of the Ottoman Empire, which began after the death of Sultan Suleiman the Magnificent in 1566 and the murder of the Grand Vezir Muhammed Sokolović in 1579. The internal decay of the Ottoman state brought about increasing corruption, insecurity, and economic decline. The Ragusans slowly but surely started withdrawing from the Balkans during the seventeenth century and investing their capital in other enterprises, particularly banking in Italy. These undertakings, however, were not adequate substitutes for the valuable Balkan market which for centuries had constituted the basis of Dubrovnik's prosperity and which was now gradually being lost.

The catastrophic earthquake of April 6, 1667, dealt a terrible blow to Dubrovnik. The lower part of the city, except for a few houses, churches, and palaces, was destroyed, and it is estimated that the deaths in Dubrovnik and its territories amounted to about 4,000 persons, including large numbers of patricians. In fact, the patriciate was so weakened that the survivors had to admit a group of ten of the richest merchant families into their ranks in order to continue to govern the city. This produced negative effects because of the reluctance of many old patricians to recognize the "new nobles" as their equals. Nevertheless, the patricians and the population as a whole showed the highest degree of courage and sacrifice in the terrible circumstances following the earthquake. They rapidly rebuilt the city and bravely resisted many attempts by the Ottomans and by the Venetians to take advantage of the catastrophe and seize control of the city. Dubrovnik continued as an independent republic.

In the eighteenth century Dubrovnik managed to achieve considerable economic progress, and its ships once again became numerous and very important on the Mediterranean. However, the patricians, small in numbers and disunited, became increasingly conservative in their views and methods. They stuck stubbornly to the old ways, which had produced excellent results in earlier centuries but were inadequate in the turbulent and rapidly changing times of the eighteenth century.

Though the ideas of the French Enlightenment success-fully penetrated the ranks of Dubrovnik's merchants and younger patricians, the ruling noblemen refused to recognize their existence. This attitude can be seen in the way Dubrov-nik acted toward the United States of America, whose struggle for freedom received widespread sympathy in the city. When the Ragusan envoy in Paris, the very able Fran-cesco Favi, suggested that the Ragusans recognize the newly created United States, the government answered, in May, 1783: "Although this Senate has considered that such a move must be made, it believes, by the same token, that it is neces-sary to make it with due circumspection and caution." There-fore, Dubrovnik would be willing to recognize the United States only when "by other princes, and particularly by the English lords, the said colonies are recognized as free and independent."

It is interesting that Favi had a prophetic vision of Amer-ica's future and wrote at length to the Ragusan government on the American Revolution, trade with the United States, and related matters. In July, 1783, Favi was writing, among other things: "The predictions made by the most illuminated politicians that, once free, America would absorb Europe begin to materialize." Speaking of massive emigration from Europe to the United States, Favi added: "This should open the eyes of the princes whose governments do not much favor arts and agriculture; if they do not adopt a better system, their states shortly will be depopulated and America perhaps will owe its growth largely to the bad governments of Europe. . . . All appearances show that that country will become the most flourishing on earth." Later, in a letter of September, 1783, Favi stressed this point once again: "At present, Americans are not too rich, but in the future their wealth will increase with their prosperity, which is beyond doubt." However, all of Favi's efforts failed to convince the Ragusan government to make a commercial treaty with the United States, a treaty that the American representatives were very eager to arrange. This was due to the gradual loss of pragmatic sense—once the principal characteristic of Ragusan diplomacy—by the governing conservative patriciate of Dubrovnik.

Throughout this period and in spite of increasing difficulties and decay, Dubrovnik produced a large number of literary men and scholars whose works attained European prominence and are very much alive even today. Among them were the famous comedist Marin Držić, 1508–67 (see Chapter V); the mathematician Marin Getaldić, 1566–1626, whose works were widely known and used in the West; the greatest Ragusan poet Djivo Gundulić, 1589–1638, author of the famous poem "Osman" and considered to be the best Slavic poet of his time; the prominent byzantinist and numismatist Anselmo Banduri, 1671–1743, whose activities in Paris brought him membership in the French Academy; and most important of all, the Jesuit Rudjer Bošković, 1711–87, a scholar, philosopher, and astronomer who was a professor in the universities of Paris and Milan, became a member of the British Royal Society, was a personal friend of Benjamin Franklin, and is today considered as one of the precursors of modern atomic physics. All of them, no matter how illustrious they became or where they lived, always remained dedicated to their homeland and contributed as much to its culture as they could.

However, Dubrovnik was not able to resist the pressure of the greatest conqueror of his day, Napoleon. The French general and later emperor, having destroyed the other glorious patrician republic, Venice, in 1797, proceeded with his expansions in various directions. This eventually brought him into Dalmatia. In 1806, when the French were supposed to fight the Russians in Boka Kotorska, south of Dubrovnik, the Ragusan government was asked to grant Napoleon's armies free passage through its territory. In spite of the opposition of some, the majority of Dubrovnik's weary and despondent patricians decided to let in the French. And so, for the first time in its long history, on May 27, 1806, a foreign army marched into Dubrovnik and stayed there. It is true that the French did not immediately do away with the republic, but the government continued to survive only as a moribund organization until, on January 31, 1808, it was abolished by a simple decree of the French commanding officer, Marshal Marmont. There were some weak attempts to re-establish the republic after Napoleon's downfall, but without results. The ancient spirit of independence survived, although Dubrovnik was incorporated into the Austrian Empire, where it remained until joining the new Yugoslav state in 1918.

Thus, paradoxically, at the time when a new, nationalistic spirit was sweeping through the Slavic lands in the Balkans, when the Serbians, after their uprising in 1804, were struggling to obtain freedom from the Ottomans, and when the Croatians were experiencing a revival of national awareness and a strengthening of ideas of their statehood, the only southern Slavic state which had remained independent for centuries crumbled under foreign intrusion and disappeared forever. However, in the more than one thousand years of its history, Dubrovnik earned a permanent and prominent place in Slavic, Mediterranean, and European history. As Jorjo Tadić wrote: "This is a city which in all the centuries of its glorious history showed incredible vitality, which almost constantly produced men of great abilities, which created invaluable works in all walks of human spirit and activity, and which, finally, is rightfully considered—not only because of its outward, natural beauty—as one of the most precious jewels that the Yugoslavs possess."

Bibliographical Essay

As was pointed out in the preface, there is no history of Dubrovnik meeting present-day standards in any language. The works on this city's past in Western languages are generally obsolete or widely scattered in various editions and periodicals. The only English history, L. Villari's *The Republic of Ragusa: An Episode of the Turkish Conquest* (1904), is no more than an uncritical recounting of local Ragusan annals and chronicles. The works by F. M. Appendini, *Notizie istorico-critiche sulle antichità, storia e letteratura de' Ragusei* (2 vols., 1802), and by J. Chr. Engel, *Geschichte des Freystaates Ragusa* (1807), also rely heavily and uncritically on chronicles and similar materials and are in many ways obsolete. Most importantly, none of these works take into consideration the enormous source material in the Ragusan archives, without which no serious history of Dubrovnik can be written. G. Gelcich, in *Dello sviluppo civile di Ragusa considerato ne' suoi monumenti storici ed artistici* (1884), gives a short but much better account of Dubrovnik's past, based on research in archival and other sources. However, this work is still far from being satisfactory.

There is a series of works by the great Viennese historian of Czech origin, C. Jireček. Some of them are directly concerned with Dubrovnik: "Der ragusanische Dichter Šiško Menčetić," *Archiv für slavische Philologie*, Vol. XVIII (1897); "Beiträge zur ragusanischen Literatursgeschichte," *ibid.*, Vol. XXI (1899); *Die Bedeutung von Ragusa in der Handelsgeschichte des Mittelalters* (1899); and "Die mittelalterliche Kanzlei der Ragusaner," *Arch. für slav. Phil.*, Vol. XXVI (1904). Other works by Jireček deal with larger subjects but give much useful information on Dubrovnik, and all of them rely heavily on Ragusan archival material. A few of these are *Die Handelsstrassen und Bergwerke von Serbien und Bosnien während des Mittelalters* (1879); *Die Romanen in den Städten Dalmatiens während des Mittelalters* (2 vols., 1901, 1903); and *Geschichte der Serben* (2 vols., 1911, 1918).

Another prominent historian of Dubrovnik and of the southern Slavs was the Ragusan Milan Rešetar, a professor in the Viennese University like Jireček. From his many articles published in Western languages we shall mention only three: "Die ragusanischen Urkunden des XIII–XV[ten] Jahrhunderts," *Arch. für slav. Phil.*, Vols. XVI (1894) and XVII (1895); "Le monete della Repubblica di Ragusa," *Rivista italiana di numismatica*, Vol. II (1905); "Das Münzwesen der Republik Ragusa," *Monatsblatt der Numismat. Gesellschaft*, No. 323–27 (1911). Let us add here the study by Karl Kovač, "Nikolaus Ragusinus und seine Zeit; Archivalische Beiträge zur Geschichte der Malerei in Ragusa im XV und der ersten Hälfte des XVI Jahrhunderts," published as an appendix to *Jahrbuch des kunsthistorichen Institutes der K.K. Zentralkommission für Denkmalpflege,* Vol. XI (1917).

More recently, several authors have published works in Western languages concerning Dubrovnik's past. In this connection let us mention the following:

Kovačević, D. "Dans la Serbie et la Bosnie médiévales: les mines d'or et d'argent," *Annales ESC,* March–April, 1960.
Krekić, B. *Dubrovnik (Raguse) et le Levant au Moyen Age.* Paris, 1961.
———. "Trois fragments concernant les relations entre Dubrovnik (Raguse) et l'Italie au XIVe siècle," *Godišnjak Filoz·fakult·u Novom Sadu,* Vol. IX (1966).
———. "Un mercante e diplomatico da Dubrovnik (Ragusa) a Venezia nel Trecento," *Studi veneziani,* Vol. IX (1967).
Mahnken, I. "Zur Frage der Dialekteigentümlichkeiten des Serbokroatischen in Dubrovnik im XIV Jahrhundert," *Opera Slavica,* Vol. IV (1963).
Popović-Radenković, M. "Le relazioni commerciali fra Dubrovnik (Ragusa) e la Puglia nel periodo angioino (1266–1442)," *Archivio storico per le Provincie napoletane,* n.s., Vols. XXXVII–XXXVIII (1957–58).
———. "La penetrazione dei mercanti pratesi a Dubrovnik (Ragusa) nella prima metà del XV secolo," *Archivio storico italiano,* Anno CVII (1959).
Skok, P. "Les origines de Raguse," *Slavia,* Vol. X (1931).
Soloviev, A. "Le patriciat de Raguse au XVe siècle," *Rešetarov zbornik* (1930).
Tadić, J. "Le port de Raguse et sa flotte au XVIe siècle," *Le*

Navire et l'Economie Maritime du Moyen-Age au XVIIIe siècle principalement en Méditerranée. Paris, 1958.

———. "Les Sources de l'histoire maritime yougoslave," *Les Sources de l'Histoire Maritime en Europe, du Moyen Age au XVIIIe siècle.* Paris, 1962.

Of course, the best works on Dubrovnik have been published in a large number of books and articles written in Serbo-Croatian by Yugoslav scholars. Before we list just a few of the books which were particularly useful in the preparation of this work, let us point out once more that, even in Serbo-Croatian, there is no satisfactory, comprehensive history of Dubrovnik. A good, though very short, survey was published by C. Jireček in Czech in *Ottuw Slovnik Naucny,* Vol. VIII. This was later translated into Serbo-Croatian as the introduction to a very valuable work by M. Rešetar, *Dubrovačka numizmatika* (*The Ragusan Numismatics*) (2 vols., Sremski Karlovci–Belgrade–Zemun, 1924, 1925).

The best comprehensive view of Ragusan history existing today is the one written by Jorjo Tadić under the titles: "Dubrovnik od postanka do kraja XV stoljeća" ("Dubrovnik from the Origins to the End of the Fifteenth Century"); "Dubrovačka Republika do početka XVIII stoljeća" ("The Ragusan Republic Until the Beginning of the Seventeenth Century"); and "Nazadovanje Dubrovnika i veliki potres" ("The Decay of Dubrovnik and the Great Earthquake"), published in *Historija naroda Jugoslavije* (*The History of the Yugoslav Peoples*), Vols. I and II (Belgrade-Zagreb, 1953, 1959).

The following is a list of books in Serbo-Croatian which were useful in the preparation of this work.

Beritić, L. *Utvrdjenja grada Dubrovnika* (*The Fortifications of the City of Dubrovnik*). Zagreb, 1955.

Božić, I. *Dubrovnik i Turska u XIV i XV veku* (*Dubrovnik and Turkey in the Fourteenth and Fifteenth Centuries*). Belgrade, 1952.

Ćirković, S. *Herceg Stefan Vukčić-Kosača i njegovo doba* (*The Herzeg Stephen Vukčić-Kosača and His Epoch*). Belgrade, 1964.

Dinić, M. *O Nikoli Altomanoviću* (*On Nikola Altomanović*). Belgrade, 1932.

————. *Za istoriju rudarstva u srednjevekovnoj Srbiji i Bosni* (*For the History of Mining in Medieval Serbia and Bosnia*). Vols. I and II. Belgrade, 1955, 1962.

Djurić, V. *Dubrovačka slikarska škola* (*The Ragusan School of Painting*). Belgrade, 1963.

Fisković, C. *Naši graditelji i kipari XV i XVI stoljeća u Dubrovniku* (*Our Fifteenth- and Sixteenth-Century Builders and Sculptors in Dubrovnik*). Zagreb, 1947.

Jeremić, R., and J. Tadić, *Prilozi za istoriju zdravstvene kulture starog Dubrovnika* (*Contributions to the History of Hygiene in old Dubrovnik*), Vols. I–III, Belgrade, 1938–1940.

Mahnken, I. *Dubrovački patricijat u XIV veku* (*The Ragusan Patriciate in the XIVth Century*), 2 vols., Belgrade, 1960.

Medini, M. *Dubrovnik Gučetića* (*Dubrovnik of the Gučetićs*). Belgrade, 1953.

THE CENTERS OF CIVILIZATION SERIES

1. *Athens in the Age of Pericles*, by Charles Alexander Robinson, Jr.

2. *Shiraz: Persian City of Saints and Poets*, by A. J. Arberry.

3. *Constantinople in the Age of Justinian*, by Glanville Downey.

4. *Fez in the Age of the Marinides*, by Roger Le Tourneau, translated from the French by Besse Alberta Clement.

5. *Rome in the Augustan Age*, by Henry Thompson Rowell.

6. *Antioch in the Age of Theodosius the Great*, by Glanville Downey.

7. *Dublin in the Age of William Butler Yeats and James Joyce*, by Richard M. Kain.

8. *Gaza in the Early Sixth Century*, by Glanville Downey.

9. *Istanbul and the Civilization of the Ottoman Empire*, by Bernard Lewis.

10. *Aix-la-Chapelle in the Age of Charlemagne*, by Richard E. Sullivan.

11. *Thebes in the Age of Amunhotep III*, by Elizabeth Riefstahl.

12. *Damascus Under the Mamlūks*, by Nicola A. Ziadeh.

13. *Chicago*, by Edward Wagenknecht.

14. *Moscow and the Roots of Russian Culture*, by Arthur Voyce.

15. *Florence in the Age of Dante*, by Paul Ruggiers.

16. *Cairo*, by Gaston Wiet, translated by Seymour Feiler.

17. *Edinburgh in the Age of Sir Walter Scott*, by Douglas Young.

18. *Bukhara*, by Richard Nelson Frye.

19. *Boston in the Age of John Fitzgerald Kennedy*, by Walter Muir Whitehill.

20. *Vienna in the Age of Franz Josef*, by Arthur J. May.

21. *Amsterdam in the Age of Rembrandt*, by John J. Murray.

22. *Kyoto in the Momoyama Period*, by Wendell Cole.

23. *London in the Age of Charles Dickens*, by Aldon D. Bell.

24. *Sardis in the Age of Croesus*, by John Griffiths Pedley.

25. *Los Angeles: A Profile*, by W. W. Robinson.

26. *Charleston in the Age of the Pinckneys*, by George C. Rogers, Jr.

27. *Antwerp in the Age of Plantin and Brueghel*, by John J. Murray.

28. *Baghdad: Metropolis of the Abbasid Caliphate*, by Gaston Wiet, translated by Seymour Feiler.

29. *Dijon and the Valois Dukes of Burgundy*, by William R. Tyler.

30. *Dubrovnik in the 14th and 15th Centuries: A City Between East and West*, by Bariša Krekić.

UNIVERSITY OF OKLAHOMA PRESS : NORMAN

The paper on which this book is printed bears the watermark of the University of Oklahoma Press and has an effective life of at least three hundred years.

University of Oklahoma Press

Norman

DATE DUE

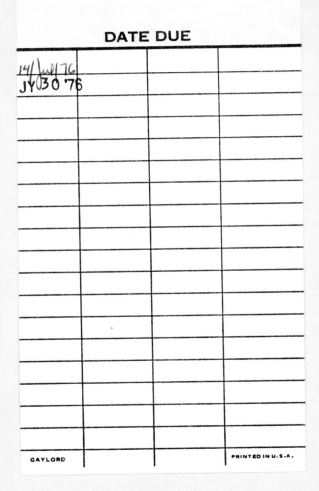

14 Jul 76			
JY 30 76			
GAYLORD			PRINTED IN U.S.A.